ARCHITECTURAL
GUIDES FOR TRAVELERS

·

CLASSICAL
TURKEY

ARCHITECTURAL
GUIDES FOR TRAVELERS

•

CLASSICAL TURKEY

JOHN FREELY

CHRONICLE BOOKS • SAN FRANCISCO

First published in the United States in 1990 by Chronicle Books.

Series conceived by Georgina Harding
Editor: Elizabeth Eyres
Series design: Clare Finlaison
Design: Wendy Bann
Maps and plans: David Woodroffe
Picture research: Emma Milne
Index: Hilary Bird

Printed in The Netherlands by Giethoorn, Meppel

Library of Congress Cataloging-in-Publication Data:
Freely, John.
    Classical Turkey / John Freely
        p.   cm. — (Architectural guides for travelers)
    ISBN 0-87701-729-8
    1. Architecture. Greek—Turkey—Guide-books.   2. Architecture
    -Turkey—Guide-books.   3. Turkey—Antiquities—Guide-books.
    I. Title   II. Series.
NA279.A8F74   1990
722'.8'09561—dc20   90-27549
                                                             CIP

10 9 8 7 6 5 4 3 2 1

Chronicle Books
275 Fifth Street
San Francisco, California 94103

CONTENTS

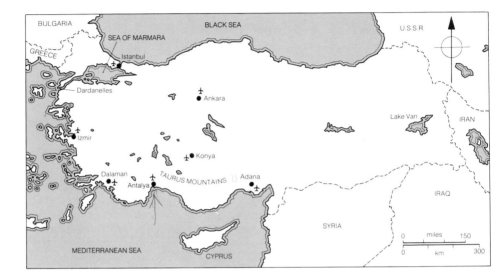

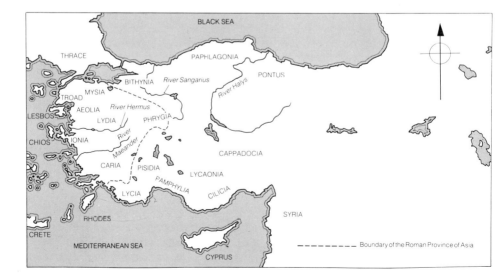

PREFACE

This book is an introduction and guide to the architecture of classical Turkey. The monuments described are those of the ancient Graeco-Roman cities in the western part of Anatolia, the subcontinent more generally known in the past as Asia Minor. Anatolia is the Asian part of modern Turkey, a country connected by geography and history to both Europe and Asia.

The European and Asian parts of Turkey are separated by the Bosphorus, the Sea of Marmara (Propontis) and the Dardanelles (Hellespont), with Thrace to the west of the straits and Anatolia to the east. The maritime boundaries of the country are the Black Sea (Euxine) on the north, the Aegean on the west, and the Mediterranean on the south. Turkey has land boundaries in Asia with the Soviet Union, Iraq, Iran and Syria, and in Europe with Bulgaria and Greece. It also has a maritime boundary with Greece. This weaves through the eastern Aegean between a series of Greek archipelagos and the Turkish shore, and extends to the southwesternmost promontories of Asia Minor, where the Aegean merges into the Mediterranean. On this incomparably beautiful and historic coastline the classical architecture of the eastern Greeks emerged, part of the flowering of a civilization that spread from Europe to Asia at the dawn of recorded history.

Most of the sites described in the chapters that follow lie on or near the Aegean and Mediterranean coasts of Turkey, though some are along the river valleys that make their way down from the great Anatolian plateau to the seas that bound Asia Minor. The time span covered here begins early in the first millennium BC and continues halfway through the first millennium of the Christian era, when the rise of Christianity in the Byzantine Empire ended the pagan Graeco-Roman culture in Greece and Asia Minor.

The principal extant monuments of classical Turkey are described in some detail, particularly in the context of the ancient Greek cities of which they were an integral part. These cities are the focal points in the nine following

(*Opposite*) Modern Turkey (*top*); ancient regions of Asia Minor (*bottom*).

vii

chapters, which each treat one of the classical regions of Asia Minor, proceeding along the Aegean and Mediterranean coasts and occasionally into the interior of the Anatolian subcontinent. The appendices provide background information for a more thorough understanding of the monuments, including outlines of their chronology and a note on classical architecture.

The chronology outlines the political history (and prehistory) of the Asian Greeks, beginning with the founding of their cities in the Dark Ages of the ancient world and ending with the destruction of Graeco-Roman civilization in the middle centuries of the first millennium AD. The periods into which this history is divided are the archaic (*c.* 750–479 BC); classical (479–323 BC); Hellenistic (323–130 BC); Roman (130 BC-AD 330); and Byzantine, the era which began in AD 330, when Constantine the Great shifted the capital of his empire from Rome to Byzantium, which thereafter came to be called Constantinople. The early Byzantine period is also occasionally referred to as 'late antiquity', which continued in Asia Minor until the last traces of Graeco-Roman civilization vanished in the eastern provinces of the Empire, leaving the magnificent ruins that can be seen today.

The sites described in this book lie on or near the Aegean and Mediterranean coasts of Turkey. The itineraries begin at Çanakkale, on the Dardanelles, and proceed from there along the coast as far as Side, with excursions to a number of sites in the interior. All of these sites can be seen in a two-week tour by car, for the coastal highways are quite good and one can easily average 80 kph (50 mph). Those with only a week's holiday would be advised to concentrate on a specific area. One possibility would be a tour of the major classical sites that can be seen on day trips from either Izmir or Kuşadasi; namely Ephesus, Priene, Miletus, Didyma, Aphrodisias, Sardis and Pergamum. Another possibility would be to visit the sites along the Mediterranean coast, the major ones being Cnidus, Telmessus, Caunus, Xanthus, Patara, Myra, Phaselis, Perge, Aspendus and Side. A third possibility is the Mavi Yol, or Blue Journey, voyages that usually begin in Bodrum, Marmaris or Fethiye and take one around the Lycian shore, the most beautiful stretch of the Turkish coast.

INTRODUCTION

Turkey is a palimpsest of civilizations, in which each successive culture is built on and from the ruins of those that
preceded it on the immemorial earth of Anatolia. Indeed,
their remains form part of the topography of Asia Minor.
Even the ruins of ancient Graeco-Roman cities stand on sites
that were inhabited since the Bronze Age on this westernmost extension of Asia. Such is the mound of Hisarlík, the
deeply layered hill on the Asian side of the Dardanelles,
which Heinrich Schliemann first explored in the summer of
1868, at the beginning of his search for Homeric Troy. As
Schliemann wrote in the following year, the site:

> fully agrees with the description Homer gives of Ilium ... The hill
> seems destined by nature to carry a great city ... there is no
> other place in the whole region to compare with it.

So Homer himself must have felt, when he too looked at this
ancient site for the first time, some five centuries after the

A view of the walls of
Troy.

1

siege that he describes in the *Iliad* and harks back upon in the *Odyssey*.

Homer's epics undoubtedly perpetuate the folk-memory of a great war that took place before the beginning of recorded Hellenic history, in which an army gathered from all the Mycenaean states in Greece besieged Troy, the most powerful city in northwestern Anatolia, at the close of the Bronze Age. The significance of the Trojan war is a much debated topic; the most prevalent opinion today is that it was part of a widespread struggle throughout Anatolia and the eastern Mediterranean in the second half of the 13th century BC, including the collapse of the Hittite Empire, the attacks of the Sea Peoples on Egypt, and the destruction of Mycenaean civilization.

About a century later, Greece came to be dominated by a warrior race called the Dorians, who may have been invaders from the north or a previously subservient indigenous people who seized power after the collapse of Mycenaean civilization. The coming to power of the Dorians forced many Hellenes to flee from their homeland to the western coast of Asia Minor and its offshore islands, beginning a new age in the history of the Greek world.

The first to move were the Aeolians, who left their homes in Thessaly, Phocis, Locris and Boeotia, *c.* 1,100 BC. They first settled on the islands of Lesbos and Tenedos, and a little later crossed over to Anatolia, where they founded settlements in the Troad (the land of Troy) and farther south, in the region that came to be called Asian Aeolis. Soon afterwards, twelve of these Aeolian cities formed a confederation known as the Aeolian League.

The Aeolians were followed early in the tenth century by the Ionians, who, according to tradition, were led to Asia Minor by a son of King Codrus of Athens. The Ionians settled on the islands of Chios and Samos and on the Anatolian mainland just below Aeolis. Their lands extended south as far as the Maeander River, where they too founded twelve cities; these became the Ionian League, known to the Greeks as the Dodecapolis. Later in the tenth century, the Dorians themselves sent an expedition across the southern Aegean, and established three cities on Rhodes, one on Cos, and two on the southwesternmost corner of the Anatolian coast, at Halicarnassus and Cnidus.

All these original settlements were on or near the Aegean

coast, but soon afterwards other Greek cities were founded inland, most of them along the valleys of the Hermus and Maeander rivers. Later still, other cities were established along the Mediterranean coast of Anatolia and up the valley of the Xanthus River. These settlements all regarded themselves as Greek cities, and throughout antiquity their institutions were purely Greek, even when they came to be dominated by the Romans.

The Greeks thus came into contact with the native peoples of western Anatolia many of whom had been displaced by the struggles that took place during the second half of the 13th century BC. These were the Mysians, Phrygians, Lydians, Carians, Lycians, Pamphylians, Pisidians and Cilicians, all of whom eventually became Hellenized, while at the same time deeply influencing the culture of the Asian Greeks.

The Asian Greek settlements were all flourishing by the second half of the eighth century BC, the dawn of the archaic period. At this time the Ionian cities on the Aegean coast led the Hellenes in sending out expeditions to establish colonies all over the Mediterranean and in the lands surrounding the Black Sea, the Greek Euxine. (The city of Miletus alone founded some 80 colonies.) In so doing they greatly expanded the boundaries of the Greek world, which in the west flourished particularly in Sicily and southern Italy, the region known in antiquity as Magna Graecia.

Simultaneously, these Ionian cities brought about an extraordinary flowering of Greek culture, which had been moribund since the collapse of Mycenaean civilization. This blossoming began with the epics of Homer, who was born in the mid-eighth century BC (his dates are very uncertain), probably in Smyrna, although Chios and other places in Ionia claimed to be his birthplace. It produced many of the first and greatest Greek poets, philosophers, physicists, physicians, mathematicians, astronomers, geographers, historians (such as Herodotus, who was born at Halicarnassus *c*. 484 BC), sculptors, painters, architects and city-planners, most of whom have won enduring fame.

The Ionian renaissance was in large part due to their expansion, which brought them into contact with older and more advanced civilizations, particularly that of the Egyptians. But their movement deeper into Anatolia also brought them into conflict with their more powerful neighbours to the east, first the Lydians and then the Persians.

The conflict began when King Gyges set out from Sardis, the Lydian capital, and invaded Ionia *c*. 665 BC. During the following century the Lydians periodically attacked the Greek cities on the Aegean coast of Asia Minor and eventually brought them under their control. Croesus, the last of the Lydian kings (561–546 BC), was a great admirer of Hellenic culture and gave extraordinarily generous presents to the Greeks, both on the mainland and in Asia Minor. But in 546 BC Croesus was defeated by King Cyrus of Persia and died in captivity shortly afterwards, with the Persians quickly occupying all of western Asia Minor and subjugating the eastern Greeks.

The Ionians, aided by the Athenians, revolted against Persian rule in 499 BC, burning Sardis and winning some initial victories in Asia Minor. But the Persians eventually crushed the Ionian Revolt in 494 BC, at the battle of Lade, after which they burned Miletus to the ground. Four years later the Persians invaded Greece, but they were defeated at the battle of Marathon. Then in 480 BC King Xerxes led the Persian army in a second invasion of Greece, in which he destroyed Athens before his fleet was defeated at the battle of Salamis later that year. The following year the Greeks were victorious over the Persians at both Plataea and Cape Mycale, permanently ending the Persian threat to Greece.

These victories marked the end of the archaic age and the start of the glorious classical period in Hellenic history. However, within a year after the victories at Plataea and Cape Mycale the Greek cities in Asia Minor were drawn into the Delian League, a naval confederation that was dominated by Athens to the extent that both ancient and modern historians refer to it as the Athenian Empire. The League was dissolved in 404 BC, following the final defeat of Athens in the Peloponnesian War, and then in 387/386 BC the Spartans abandoned the Asian Greeks to the Persians in a treaty called the King's Peace. That there was very little building in Asia Minor during the classical period was probably due to the uncertain status of the Asian Greeks, who at this time were taxed unmercifully by Athens and still dominated by the Persians, even when not directly under Persian rule.

Alexander the Great freed the Asian Greeks from Persian domination at the beginning of his invasion of Asia in 334 BC, but this only put them under Macedonian rule. Alexander's death in 323 BC brought the classical period to a close and

Head of Alexander the Great from Pergamum; first half of the 2nd century BC.

marked the beginning of the Hellenistic period. During the next half century Alexander's successors, the Diadochoi, allowed several independent states to emerge in Asia Minor, the most notable being Pergamum. The Pergamene Kingdom came to an end in 133 BC, when its last ruler bequeathed his realm to Rome. Three years later the Romans organized most of western Anatolia into the Province of Asia, beginning the Roman period in the history of Asia Minor.

Many of the remarkable cultural achievements of the archaic and classical periods were recorded by Herodotus, among them being the construction by the Ionians of the two largest temples ever erected in the Greek world, the Heraeum of Samos and the Artemisium of Ephesus. The first of these was built *c.* 570–560 BC by two Samians, Rhoecus and Theodorus, who were renowned craftsmen as well as architects. With them begins the recorded history of classical architecture, for Theodorus of Samos was the first to write a book on the subject, a work now lost but mentioned by Vitruvius in his *De architectura (The Ten Books of Architecture)*. Shortly after the completion of the Heraeum, Theodorus assisted in the design of the Artemisium of Ephesus.

These colossal monuments were the climax of a development that began with the Greek temples of the early archaic period. The first monumental Greek temples were erected in the seventh century BC, virtually simultaneously in mainland Greece, Magna Graecia and Asia Minor, for the Hellenes maintained a cultural unity that transcended the separations of their diaspora. From the beginning Greek architects concentrated their efforts on the temple. The core of the temple was the simple, rectangular, central room of the shrine, the *cella*, which often had an inner sanctum, the *naiskos*, designed to shelter a cult-statue or a sacred icon, the *xoanon*. The architects then surrounded the cella with a *pteron*, or colonnade, which served a decorative purpose and sheltered worshippers at the temple.

The great architectural orders, the Doric and the Ionic, were chiefly developed in the design and decoration of this pteron. Both orders were fully developed by the sixth century BC, attaining the height of their refinement in the following century. The Doric order first appeared in lands occupied by the Dorians and predominated in mainland Greece and Magna Graecia, while the Ionic was dominant in Asia Minor and on the islands of the eastern Aegean, precisely where the Ionians had settled during their migration to the east.

The different origins of the two orders can perhaps be traced through their capitals. The Doric order may derive from Mycenaean capitals that survived into the archaic period at Mycenae. The Ionic order was undoubtedly influenced by the long acquaintance of the Ionians with Egypt, though it is not clear whether the palm-leaf capitals of Asian Aeolis, which are probably of Egyptian origin, developed into the final form of the Ionic capital. The Corinthian order did not predominate until the Roman period and was

A Corinthian capital.

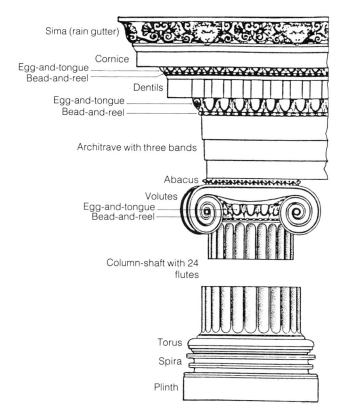

Sima (rain gutter)

Cornice
Egg-and-tongue
Bead-and-reel

Dentils

Egg-and-tongue
Bead-and-reel

Architrave with three bands

Abacus

Volutes
Egg-and-tongue
Bead-and-reel

Column-shaft with 24
flutes

Torus

Spira

Plinth

The Ionic order of the
Temple of Athena
Polias, Priene.

really only a variation of the Ionic, the essential difference being the substitution of the acanthus capital for the Ionic volutes. One of the earliest Corinthian temples is that of Zeus Olbius at Olba-Diocaesarea in Cilicia erected early in the third century BC.

The Ionic order continued to dominate architecture in Asia Minor from the archaic period up until the beginning of the Roman era. The most influential architects during that time were Pythius, who lived in the fourth century BC, and Hermogenes, who flourished c. 200 BC. Both architects were from Priene and wrote books about their edifices, that survive only through paraphrases in Vitruvius. Pythius was one of the architects of the Mausoleum at Halicarnassus, which ranked with the Artemisium at Ephesus as one of the Seven Wonders of the Ancient World; his other extant work is the Temple of Athena Polias at Priene. Hermogenes was the great theoretician of classical architecture: he codified

The Temple of Athena
Polias, Priene.

rules for the Ionic order in books that profoundly influenced
Vitruvius and, through him, the architecture of Europe from
the Renaissance onwards. His two extant works are the
Temple of Dionysus at Teos and the Temple of Artemis
Leucophryne at Magnesia-ad-Maeandrum.

Among the few buildings constructed in the classical
period were those of a funerary nature. The Mausoleum at
Halicarnassus, completed *c.* 351 BC, emerged from a
tradition of funerary architecture that had its origins in both
western Greece and Asia Minor, particularly among the
Hellenized Carians and Lycians. But the most extraordinary
extant example of this tradition is the Nereid Monument from
Xanthus, built in the late fifth century BC. Both the Mausoleum
and the Nereid Monument were built in the Ionic order, and
are renowned not only for the uniqueness of their architecture but also for the sculptures with which they were

adorned. Other, less monumental, examples of funerary architecture stand on their original sites, principally in the cities of ancient Lycia.

The development of architecture during the Hellenistic period was profoundly influenced by Pergamum, the most important classical site in northwestern Anatolia. Under the brilliant dynasty of the Attalids, Pergamum was the capital of the most powerful kingdom that emerged in western Asia Minor during this period, and rivalled both Athens and Alexandria as a centre of Greek culture, particularly in architecture and sculpture. It continued to flourish under Roman rule, when its sanctuary of the healing-god Asclepius made it one of the most important shrines in the Roman Empire.

The history of Pergamum is reflected in its architecture, the most famous example of which is the great Altar of Zeus, built in the Hellenistic period. During the Roman period the Pergamenes made frequent use of the Corinthian order in their buildings, but at the same time they developed their own palm-leaf capital, the Pergamene, which may derive from the Aeolic capital. The Pergamene kings also built monumental edifices in other cities, the most famous being the *stoas*, or porticoes, of Eumenes II and Attalus II in Athens.

A Pergamene capital.

Other classical sites in Asia Minor reflect their different histories in the architecture of their surviving monuments. Ephesus, the largest and most prosperous city in Asia Minor during the Imperial Roman era, is largely a Roman city, with few notable monuments from its earlier period. It was the principal port and commercial centre on the Aegean coast, with a population that reached 400,000 during the second century AD. Ephesus was also the most popular place of pilgrimage in the Graeco-Roman world at that time because it contained the shrine of Ephesian Artemis. Priene, on the other hand, which dates almost entirely from the late classical and early Hellenistic periods, is a quintessentially Greek city. Its architecture reflects the fact that its mountain-side site high above the Maeander plain kept it out of the mainstream of commerce during the Roman period.

Despite their differences in size and in the period of their architecture, Priene and Ephesus are examples of the Hellenic *polis*, the Greek city-state that emerged in the Dark Age that followed the collapse of Mycenaean civilization at the end of the Bronze Age. Although the most renowned edifice in each of these cities was its principal temple, that of Athena in Priene and the Artemisium in Ephesus, the core of the *polis* was the *prytaneum*, or town hall, where the routine administrative work was done. This structure preserved the archives of the city and the sacred flame that burned eternally at the shrine of Hestia, goddess of the hearth, the fire representing the continuity of the tribe and the soul of the *polis*. Another important edifice was the *bouleuterion*, or council house, which traditionally took the form of a small covered theatre with an altar as its focal point, again emphasizing the deep religious nature of the *polis* even in its political activities.

The commercial activities of the *polis* centred on the *agora*, a market area and civic centre surrounded by stoas, which housed shops and other commercial enterprises. Within the market square there was always a small temple or shrine, because commercial activities were also governed by the religio-civic laws of the *polis*.

Education in its broadest sense was provided in the gymnasium, which had facilities for both intellectual and physical training. Cultural activities centred on the theatre, which often had a small temple dedicated to Dionysus, whose cult had given rise to Greek drama. Many cities also had a library, invariably containing a shrine of Athena, who was worshipped as the goddess of learning as well as the divine protectress of the *polis*; some also had an *odeum*, a small covered theatre for musical performances; and a few had an amphitheatre, generally used for spectacles such as gladiatorial combat.

All these various institutions were grouped in a characteristic manner, with the principal temple, prytaneum, bouleuterion and agora forming the civic centre, and the other buildings arranged around them: the gymnasium and the stadium usually stood farther out from the centre, and the theatre was usually located wherever a convenient hillside would lend itself to the construction of an auditorium. Topography was all-important in the siting and laying out of a *polis*, particularly when the Greeks were establishing completely new cities such as those in Asia Minor and Magna Graecia. The Ionian cities, in particular, were founded on promontories, with harbours on both sides of a peninsula to provide alternate havens for shipping when the wind shifted. They also had an *acropolis*, or upper city, from where the populace could defend themselves when attacked by their enemies, and a line of defence walls which extended from the hilltop citadel to enclose the whole of the *polis*. The new cities of the Asian Greeks were laid out on a rectangular grid-plan; a development associated with Hippodamus of Miletus who was born *c*. 500 BC. However, recent archaeological evidence indicates that some of the earliest grid plans (dating from the seventh century BC) are to be found in the Greek colonies in Sicily.

The Greek *polis* had a clearly defined sense of its identity, expressed in the arrangement and definition of its various activities. But the sense of cultural superiority of the Asian Greeks, who saw themselves as outposts and beacons of the civilization of their race, is also reflected in the architecture of their cities, still magnificent even in their ruins.

The eventual destruction of the Greek cities of Asia Minor is most dramatically visible in the largest and most famous of them, Ephesus, whose later history is part of the chronicle of the decline of the Roman Empire and the rise of Christianity. In AD 262 the Goths attacked Ephesus and wrecked the Temple of Artemis. It was partially restored on a smaller scale during the reign of Diocletian (AD 285–305), and remained in use until 392 when Theodosius I issued an edict closing down all the pagan shrines in the empire. The temple was then destroyed in 401 by a mob led by John Chrysostom, Patriarch of Constantinople, who saw this as the final triumph of Christianity over paganism. By that time a large public building in Ephesus had been converted into a church dedicated to the Virgin Mary, as Christianity replaced the worship of the deities of the Graeco-Roman world.

Those Greek cities in western Asia Minor that had been centres of classical culture continued to exist until as late as the early seventh century, though by that time their brilliance had been considerably dimmed. But then they were all destroyed in a very brief period of time — Ephesus, Sardis and the other principal cities of the region were sacked and ruined in 616 during an invasion led by the Sassanid king Chosroes II. Many of these once-great cities disappeared from history for more than a thousand years, until their virtually abandoned ruins were rediscovered by European travellers in Anatolia, which was, by then, the heartland of the Ottoman Empire.

The first western scholar to explore the ruins of classical

Column fragment
from the Temple of
Hadrian, Cyzicus.

Asia Minor was Cyriacus of Ancona (*c*. 1391–*c*. 1453).
Cyriacus explored the Asian coast of the Sea of Marmara
just prior to the conquest of Constantinople by the Ottoman
Turks in 1453, and in the ancient Mysian city of Cyzicus,
discovered a temple built by Hadrian. He recorded that the
temple was 'undamaged and intact, almost in its original
splendour', but it has now virtually disappeared.

During the Ottoman period, a small but increasing
number of travellers managed to make their way to Asia
Minor to explore and study the ruined cities there, with the
expedition of Richard Chandler (sponsored by the Society of

Dilettanti) in 1765–6 being one of the most ambitious. When Chandler visited Sardis he recorded that it had degenerated into a 'miserable village', and when he came to Ephesus he wrote of how he wandered through the scattered ruins in search of the Artemisium:

> to as little purpose as the travellers who had preceded us … We now seek in vain for the temple; the city is prostrate: and the goddess gone.

The first systematic exploration of Asia Minor began in 1811, when Captain Beaufort of the British Royal Navy mapped the Mediterranean coast of Turkey, identifying some of the ancient sites there. This was followed by a number of other archaeological expeditions, including Charles Fellows' explorations of Lycia in 1838–44. But the most dramatic find was Heinrich Schliemann's rediscovery of Troy in excavations that began in 1870. Since then, most of the ancient Graeco-Roman cities in Asia Minor have been unearthed and studied, at least to some extent. The more famous of them, such as Pergamum, Ephesus, Sardis and Aphrodisias, are now the subjects of large-scale excavations and restorations that have recreated a fragmentary image of their former splendours. Though many of these classical sites have been excavated and restored, some of the more remote ones remain as they were when time stopped for them at the close of antiquity, so that they seem part of the lost landscape that Homer called 'the country of dreams.'

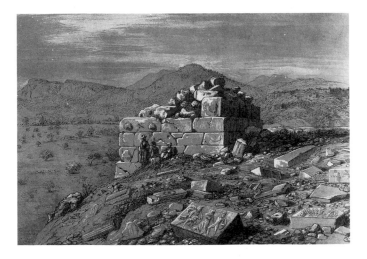

The site of the Nereid Monument at Xanthus; drawing by G. Scharf (who accompanied Fellows to Xanthus).

THE TROAD
AND AEOLIA

The Troad, or the land of Troy, forms the northwesternmost projection of the Asia Minor subcontinent. It is a huge, blunt peninsula bounded on its north by the Dardanelles, on its west by the Aegean, and on the south by the Gulf of Edremit; on its eastern side it merges into the region known in antiquity as Mysia.

The best approach to the Troad is by the car-ferry from Istanbul, an all-day journey that takes one across the Sea of Marmara to Çanakkale, the main port on the Asian shore of the Dardanelles, the Greek Hellespont. The army of Xerxes crossed the Hellespont between Abydus and Sestus in 480 BC, at the beginning of the second and last Persian invasion of Greece.

The site of ancient Troy is 27 km (17 miles) beyond Çanakkale on the Asian side of the Dardanelles, approached by a turn-off from the highway to Izmir. Before setting out from Çanakkale one might pay a visit to the museum there, which has, among other things, a few antiquities from the collection of Frank Calvert, the man who convinced Schliemann that Troy was to be found under the great mound at Hisarlík, the old Turkish name for the site.

Some travellers express disappointment at their first sight of Troy, for the site is now just a shapeless hill deeply scarred by the great trench that Schliemann cut into it, with the debris of three millennia of human existence scattered around the archaeological zone. But its old romance is still there, particularly when one stands at the top of the hill and looks out across the windy plane, with the sky-blue waters of the Dardanelles dramatically visible to the right. Homer must have stood here too when he plotted out the topography of the *Iliad*, having the Greeks beach their black-hulled ships just inside the promontory now known as Kum Kale, the Sand Castle, which marks the entrance to the Hellespont on the Asian side. The Greeks set up their camp at the northern end of the Trojan plain, and it was from here that the fighting

TROY

(*Opposite*) Fragments of the Temple of Apollo Smintheus, Chryse.

during the Trojan War surged back and forth to the great fortress-city whose ruins still dominate the landscape, more than 3,000 years later.

The excavations of Schliemann and his successors have revealed that the Hisarlík mound was first settled *c*. 3,000 BC and it remained inhabited up until the late Roman era. Nine main levels of habitation have been identified, most of which have several sub-strata, and a total of 46 levels have been documented. The lowest and earliest level is Troy I, which dates from the Bronze Age (3,000–2,500 BC), and the latest is Troy IX, the Novum Ilium of the Roman era. Archaeologists now generally agree that the Homeric city of the Iliad is Troy VIIA, which is dated to 1,275–1,240 BC. The earliest Greek artifacts were unearthed in Troy VIII, which appears to have been founded *c*. 700 BC by Aeolian colonists from Lesbos or Tenedos, who at that time established other settlements along the Aegean coast of the Troad. The city they founded at Hisarlík came to be known as Ilion, or in Latin as Ilium, venerated throughout the Graeco-Roman world as the successor of ancient Troy.

The most important monument of Ilion is the Temple of Athena, whose ruins were found in the northeast quarter of the mound. A temple of Athena is mentioned by Homer in the *Iliad*, but that is just a literary invention, for the Homeric siege of Troy is set some five centuries before the first Greek settlement on the site. The Temple of Athena at Ilion is also mentioned by Herodotus, who in Book VII of his *Histories* records that Xerxes made a pilgrimage there just before he crossed the Hellespont, sacrificing a thousand oxen as an offering to 'the Trojan Athena'.

It is recorded that Alexander the Great visited Troy immediately after he crossed the Hellespont, at the beginning of his invasion of Asia in the spring of 334 BC. Strabo writes that Alexander vowed to rebuild the Temple of Athena at Troy, and that this promise was fulfilled by Lysimachus, one of the Diadochoi, or successors of Alexander, who became ruler of Thrace after Alexander's death in 323 BC. The new Temple of Athena built by Lysimachus was in the Doric order, as demonstrated by the fragments that Schliemann found in the debris of the Hilarlík mound.

Troy was also a place of pilgrimage for the Romans, because of the myth that Rome had been founded by Aeneas, the only surviving son of King Priam of Troy. Julius

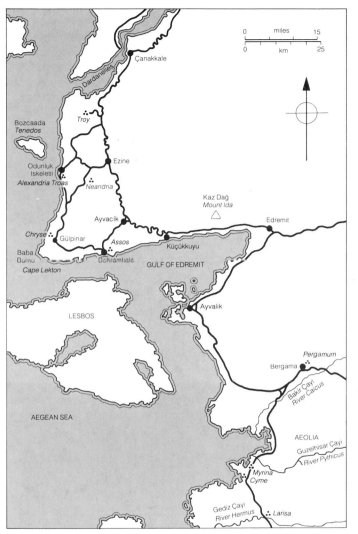

The Troad and Aeolia.

Caesar, who believed himself to be a direct descendant of Aeneas, visited Troy and gave the city immunity from taxation. The whole city of Troy was rebuilt during the reign of Augustus (27 BC-AD 14); at that time the entire top of the mound was levelled to enlarge the sacred enclosure of Athena's temple, which was then completely rebuilt once again, though using many architectural elements from the Hellenistic structure.

The bouleuterion, dating from Roman times, is just to the east of the Skaian Gate, which Schliemann identified as the main point of entry to the Homeric city from the many references to it in the *Iliad*. This was the portal through which the Trojans passed when they went out to do battle with the Achaeans, the name by which Homer refers to the Mycenaeans led by Agamemnon. These same references led Schliemann to identify the rampart on the west side of the gate as the Great Tower of Ilium. As described in the *Iliad*, this was where King Priam and the other Trojan elders stood to observe the fighting down below on the Trojan plain.

The Izmir highway continues past the turn-off to Troy and heads down through the heart of the Troad, taking one over the western foothills of Mount Ida towards the Gulf of Edremit. The modern highway follows the same course as the ancient route through the Troad, a highroad laid down soon after the establishment of the Roman Province of Asia in 129 BC. This is one of the loveliest landscapes in northwestern Asia Minor, with a vernal patchwork of small farms fringed by groves of valonia oaks stretching southwards from the Trojan plain towards the looming massif of Ida, the great mountain from which Zeus and Hera occasionally watched the fighting during the siege of Troy.

NEANDRIA

Plan of the Aeolic temple at Neandria.

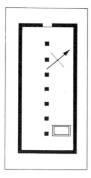

At Ezine, 25 km (16 miles) beyond the turn-off to Troy, a road to the right signposted for ancient Alexandria Troas leads out to Odunluk Iskelesi, a tiny port that serves the Aegean island of Bozcaada, known to the Greeks as Tenedos. A kilometre or so along this road one can see off to the left the mountaintop site of ancient Neandria, which is not signposted and is virtually inaccessible without a local guide.

Neandria was founded by Aeolian settlers in the sixth century BC; it remained inhabited until the end of the fourth century BC, when it was abandoned by its inhabitants in favour of the new city of Alexandria Troas. Neandria is still surrounded by its mighty defence walls of the fifth century BC; these are 3 m (9¾ ft) thick and some 3,200 m (3,500 yd) in length, and are among the most impressive fortifications of their period that have survived in western Anatolia. There are also some remnants of a polygonal defence wall of the archaic period, probably dating from the time of the original settlement.

Neandria was excavated in 1899 by the German archaeologist Robert Koldewey, who discovered the remains of an Aeolic temple dating from the end of the seventh century BC or the beginning of the following century. This is one of the oldest extant temples in Asia Minor, and the only Aeolic edifice that has survived other than in scattered fragments. The temple consisted solely of a cella on a podium, with a single row of seven wooden columns along the longitudinal axis of the building. The columns were surmounted by handsome Aeolic capitals, now on exhibit in the Istanbul Archaeological Museum. They are labelled as Proto-Ionic in the museum, but some authorities maintain they are a local variant developed in Asian Aeolis, and not a direct link in the development of Ionic capitals.

Aeolic capital from the temple at Neandria.

ALEXANDRIA TROAS

Haltway along the road from Ezine to Odunluk Iskelesi, a distance of about 10 km (6 miles), one begins to see the vast ruins of Alexandria Troas, the ancient metropolis of the Troad, now completely overgrown with shrubbery and valonia oaks, the scattered sarcophagi of its great necropolis giving it the appearance of a wrecked city of the dead. At Odunluk Iskelesi the road turns south along the coast, and after a kilometre or so it brings one to the turn-off for Dalyan. This is a tiny seaside hamlet that in Ottoman times developed around the silted-up port of Alexandria Troas, where a line of broken monoliths lie in the shallows along the sandy beach of the village's crescent cove.

According to Strabo, the original settlement on this site was called Sigia; this was probably founded early in the archaic period by Aeolians from Tenedos, for this stretch of the coast was known as the Tenedean Pieria. A new and far larger city was founded on the same site *c.* 310 BC by a successor of Alexander, Antigonus I, who named it Antigonia. After the defeat and death of Antigonus at the battle of Ipsus in 302 BC, Lysimachus changed the name of the city to Alexandria, one of fifteen cities named after Alexander by the generals who succeeded to his empire. But travellers, even in ancient times, were led by the proximity of Troy to call the city Alexandria Troas. During the Hellenistic era Alexandria Troas became the wealthiest and most populous city in the Troad, for its strategic position near the entrance to the Hellespont made it a convenient place for the trans-

The Roman baths at Alexandria Troas, from Richard Chandler's *Travels in Asia Minor, 1764–5*, (*top*); the baths today (*bottom*).

shipment of goods passing between the northern Aegean and the interior of Asia Minor.

During the reign of Augustus a colony of Roman merchants was established within the city, a community that reached the height of its wealth and influence during the reign of Hadrian. At this time the Province of Asia was

administered from Alexandria Troas by Herodes Atticus, whose magnificent odeum under the Athenian acropolis still bears his name. The principal extant monuments in Alexandria Troas were erected by Herodes during his term of office here. The most notable of these is the enormous Roman baths known locally as Bal Saray, the Honey Palace, which is dated *c*. AD 135. This is now a shapeless ruin, its great vaulted halls having for centuries served as a quarry. The architectural plan of the baths has never been determined, but it is thought that the structure resembled a classical Greek gymnasium more than the Roman thermae. Also remarkable are the well-preserved defence walls, which date from the early Hellenistic period.

The shore road that passes Dalyan and the seaward ruins of Alexandria Troas goes on around the southernmost promontory of the Troad, Baba Burnu, the Cape Lekton of the Greeks. Thirty-six km (22 miles) beyond Dalyan the road brings one to Gülpínar, the nearest village to the cape, which is approached by a rough dirt track. Just beyond the village on the way out to the cape one comes to the ruins of Chryse, a remote and romantic site which is rarely visited by outsiders.

CHRYSE

The remains of an Ionic temple of the mid-third century BC are all that is left of ancient Chryse. The temple was first excavated by the Society of Dilettanti in 1866, and has been studied again very recently by Turkish archaeologists. All that remains of the temple are its *stylobate* (the upper step, or platform) and some columns, and other architectural elements. It has been identified as a Sanctuary of Apollo Smintheus, the Mouse God, whose ancient shrine is known to have been at Chryse.

The Smintheum at Chryse is mentioned five times in the first book of the *Iliad*, for this was the home of Chryseis, the captive mistress of Agamemnon, whose kidnapping from Apollo's sanctuary brought down upon the Greeks the awesome anger of the Mouse God. Strabo mentions that the temple had a remarkable wooden cult-statue of Apollo, in which the god was represented with a mouse under his foot. The work was carved by the great sculptor Scopas, who was born on the Aegean island of Paros *c*. 420 BC.

ASSOS

Beyond Gülpínar the shore curves around the base of Cape Lekton to head east along the shore of the Gulf of Edremit; then 26 km (16 miles) beyond Chryse it brings one to Behramkale, a picturesque seaside hamlet dominated by the ruins of ancient Assos on the steep acropolis-hill above the tiny port.

The ruins of Assos were excavated in 1881–3 by the American archaeologists J. T. Clarke and F. H. Bacon. Most of the works of art and architectural remains found in this excavation have been on exhibit for more than a century at the Boston Museum of Fine Arts. Other antiquities from the site are in the Louvre and the Istanbul Archaeological Museum. Thus Assos is well known to those interested in archaeology, although the site is seldom visited by travellers.

The American excavation revealed that the acropolis at Assos was first occupied in the late Bronze Age. But the city itself dates from the seventh century BC, when, according to Strabo, a colony was established here by Aeolian settlers from Methymna on Lesbos. The most illustrious period in the history of Assos came in the years 355–341 BC, when it was the capital of a Mysian principality ruled by Hermias, the Tyrant of Atarneus. Hermias had been a student at the Platonic Academy in Athens, and when he came to power in Assos he founded a new philosophical school there. After Plato's death in 348 BC, Hermias was joined in Assos by several members of the Academy, including Aristotle, Theophrastus, Callisthenes and Xenocrates, and thus, for a brief period, the city became one of the most brilliant centres of culture in the Greek world. This period ended in 341 BC when Hermias was captured and executed by the Persians and the philosophers he had gathered around him left Assos, with Aristotle and Theophrastus crossing over to Lesbos to continue their scientific researches there.

The most impressive remains of ancient Assos are its defence walls, most of which date from the mid-fourth century BC, probably from the time of Hermias. Those walls were originally almost 5 km (3 miles) in circumference, of which almost half of the circuit is still standing, principally on the western side of the city and around the citadel on the acropolis. The modern road passes through the western walls at what was once the main gateway of Assos. This was the entrance to the lower part of the ancient city, which lay below the precipitous acropolis-hill to the south, on the more gradual slope leading down to the harbour. The structures that have been identified in the lower city include a gymnasium, just inside the west gate; the theatre, which overlooked the harbour, and above that a group of buildings that surrounded the agora. This square was bordered on its long north and south sides by stoas; on its west by the agora temple; and on its east by the bouleuterion, or council house. The most striking remains in the lower city are the huge sarcophagi in the necropolis below the southeast side of the acropolis.

The peak of the acropolis-hill is still surrounded by fragments of its ancient citadel. The only standing monument is an abandoned Ottoman mosque, its walls built from the stones of the Doric Temple of Athena, the principal monument of ancient Assos. Clarke and Bacon excavated the stylobate of the temple and carried away to Boston the surviving fragments of its frieze and some architecural elements, leaving the bare foundations and some scattered column drums and capitals. Turkish archaeologists have recently re-erected part of the peripteral colonnade, including five columns surmounted by their original Doric capitals.

Archaeological studies indicate that the Temple of Athena had a peripteral colonnade with six columns at each end and thirteen along the sides; in its front porch there were also two columns *in antis*. Built in the mid-sixth century BC, it is the only archaic Doric temple known to have been erected east of the Aegean. But it is a very odd Doric temple indeed, with a number of features showing a strong Ionic influence, as might be expected from its location here on the coast just north of Ionia. The most unusual of these features was its sculptural decoration, for in addition to the reliefs on its metopes, its architrave too was sculptured, treated as if it were an Ionic frieze.

The view from the acropolis is magnificent, particularly to the south, where the northern promontory of Lesbos is less than 8 km (5 miles) away across the strait that forms the southern boundary of the Troad. The western end of the Lesbian shore facing the Troad is the site of ancient Methymna, now the Greek village of Molivos. From here, the Aeolian colonists who founded Assos set out, twenty-seven centuries ago, crossing the strait to begin a new life on this westernmost peninsula of Asia Minor.

From Behramkale the road takes one back to the main highway at Ayvacík, an 18-km (11 mile) drive. Then from there the highway curves all the way round the Gulf of Edremit to Ayvalik, a charming seaside town that looks out through the beautiful little archipelago of offshore islets towards the eastern side of Lesbos, whose blue-green mountains seems to rise directly out of the turquoise Aegean. The highway then continues down along the coast opposite Lesbos as far as the delta of the Bakír Çayi, the River Caicus

The Temple of Athena, Assos (*right*); a restoration of the front of the temple (*below*).

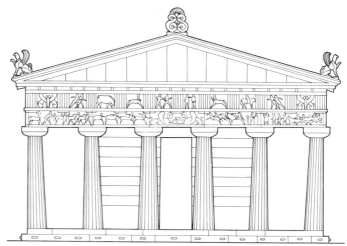

of the Greeks, where one enters the region known in antiquity as Aeolis.

Asian Aeolis extended south along the coast from the Caicus to Smyrna, the city now known as Izmir. Most of the Aeolians who settled here crossed over from Lesbos at the end of the second millennium BC, and were the first wave of the great population movement that led to the Hellenization of the Aegean coast of Asia Minor. Here, as elsewhere on the northern Aegean coast, the settlers found that the country was already inhabited by indigenous Anatolian peoples, whom they called Pelasgians and Lelegians, who apparently vanished without a trace after the Hellenic migrations.

According to Herodotus, the Aeolians founded a dozen colonies south of the Adramyttene Gulf, the most notable being Smyrna, which they later lost to the Ionians. Another renowned Aeolian city was Cyme, which, together with Chalcis and Eretria, founded the city of Cumae in 757 BC, the first Greek colony on the Italian mainland, beginning the history of Magna Graecia. The Cymaeans later founded a colony on the Pamphylian coast of Asia Minor, at Side.

Apart from Smyrna and Cyme, the other ten cities of the Aeolian League made virtually no mark on history. This is probably because the northern settlers, other than the Cymeans, were mostly farmers and herdsmen, whereas the other Greeks to their south were seafarers and merchants who came in contact with a much broader world. While the Ionians made their indelible mark on history, the Aeolians simply settled for the good life on their farms, for their lands were more fertile than those to the south. As Athenaeus writes in his *Doctors at Dinner*, completed in AD 192, the Aeolians were much 'given to wine, women, and luxurious living'. This is probably why they left no monuments along the coast where they lived throughout antiquity, their cities having vanished almost without a trace, other than a few column drums and other fragments lying along the shore.

PERGAMUM

Northwest of the Aeolian coast, up the valley of the Caicus, is the most famous site that has survived from ancient Mysia — Pergamum. The name of the ancient city is perpetuated by that of Bergama, the Turkish name for the town that emerged on the lower part of the site early in the Ottoman period.

The modern town of Bergama is built around Roman Pergamum, whereas the magnificent ruins of the Hellenistic city are high on the acropolis to its north. This gigantic spire of rock rises precipitously from the plain on three sides, with the River Selinus flowing around the base of the mountain to the west and the Cetius to its east, creating the natural fortress that first attracted settlers to this superb site.

(*Opposite*) The theatre and theatre terrace at Pergamum, with the Temple of Dionysus in the foreground.

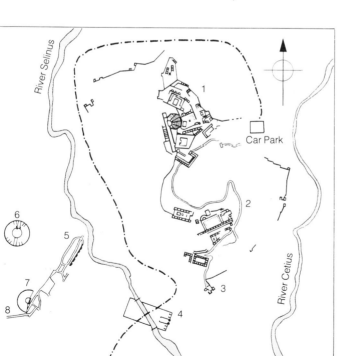

Site plan of Pergamum.
1. upper city;
2. middle city;
3. Gate of Eumenes;
4. Temple of Serapis;
5. stadium;
6. amphitheatre;
7. theatre; 8. ancient road leading to the Asclepieum.

The oldest pottery shards found at Pergamum date to the eighth century BC; these remains indicate that the first settlers on the acropolis were not Greeks, but perhaps an indigenous Anatolian people who had settled there before the Ionian and Aeolian migrations. But all the edifices on the acropolis date from the brilliant period of the Attalid era (281-133 BC), when Pergamum was the most powerful state in Asia Minor, rivalling Athens and Alexandria as a centre of Greek culture.

At the height of its power, in the first half of the second century BC, Pergamum was the capital of a kingdom that comprised most of western Anatolia, all of which became part of the Roman Province of Asia in 129 BC. During the Imperial Roman era, which began when Octavian became Augustus in 27 BC, Pergamum's population grew to over 300,000, as the city spread out from its original mountain-top site and expanded south-southwest across the Caicus plain, much as the Turkish town of Bergama does today.

Pergamum emerged as an independent state during the wars of the Diadochoi, Alexander's successors. When Lysimachus won control of northwestern Asia Minor he appointed Philetaerus, son of a Macedonian named Attalus, to govern the city of Pergamum and to safeguard his kingdom's treasury there. By the end of 281 BC Philetaerus had established himself as the ruler of a small state which originally comprised little more than the Caicus valley. His greatest achievement was the successful defence of Pergamum against the Gauls in the years 278-276 BC.

Philetaerus was succeeded in turn by Eumenes I (263-241 BC), Attalus I (241-197 BC), Eumenes II (197-159 BC), Attalus II (159-138 BC) and Attalus III (138-133 BC). Attalus I and Eumenes II also won notable victories over the Gauls, permanently stemming the advance of these barbarian invaders. In 189 BC Eumenes II and the Roman general Scipio Africanus defeated Antiochus III at the battle of Magnesia, after which Pergamum gained control of all of the former Seleucid territory in Asia Minor. Pergamum reached the peak of its greatness at this time, with a renowned school of sculpture and a famous library, rivalling Athens and Alexandria as a centre of Hellenic culture. This golden age came to an end in 133 BC with the death of Attalus III, who bequeathed his kingdom to Rome. The Romans then included Pergamum and all of its former dominions within their Province of Asia, beginning a new era in the history of Asia Minor.

The ruins on the peak of the acropolis comprise the very oldest part of Pergamum. During the Attalid period (281–133 BC) the citadel enclosed the royal palace, the theatre, the arsenal and several of the city's most important religious shrines. These institutions give this quarter a sacred and ceremonial aura, in contrast to the more plebian character of the lower city.

The gateway to the citadel on the acropolis was at its southeastern end. Just before one enters this gateway, on the left, are the well-preserved remains of a **heroum** (1), the shrine of a hero. This is a peristyle building, that is, with a surrounding colonnade, and is probably dedicated to Attalus I and Eumenes II, who after their deaths were raised to the status of heroes. One then passes through the remains of the **propylon** (2), the monumental gateway to the citadel on the acropolis, erected by Eumenes II. On the right of the propylon are the fortifications that extended from the gateway around the eastern, northern and northwestern sides of the citadel, which was left open along the remainder of its periphery because of the natural protection afforded by the precipitous slope of the acropolis rock on that side. These walls date back to the beginning of the Pergamene kingdom, with repairs made in the Byzantine era.

Inside the propylon an ancient street leads out to the north end of the narrowing citadel. At the beginning of this road, on the right, are the ruins of two **royal palaces** (3), of which just the foundations and re-assembled stacks of architectural elements remain, arrayed around the periphery of each structure. Both palaces were of the peristyle type; the first is attributed to Eumenes II and the second to Attalus I. Beyond the palaces on the right side of the street are first the remains of a complex of **Hellenistic houses** (4), and then a **barracks** and **defence tower** (5); all these structures were undoubtedly used by the garrison of the citadel, whose **arsenal** (6) formed a walled enclosure at the long and narrow northern end of the acropolis.

The principal sanctuaries of the upper city are all on the precipitous western side of the acropolis, arranged in an arc above the theatre. At the northern sector of this arc is the

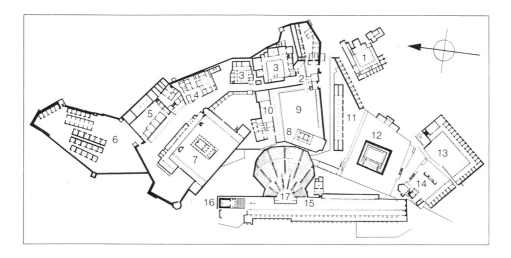

Plan of the upper city.
1. heroum;
2. propylon; 3. royal palaces; 4. Hellenistic houses; 5. barracks and defence tower;
6. arsenal;
7. Trajaneum;
8. Temple of Athena Polias; 9. temenos of Athena; 10. library;
11. Hellenistic stoa;
12. Altar of Zeus;
13. agora; 14. agora temple; 15. theatre terrace; 16. Temple of Dionysus;
17. theatre.

newly restored and magnificent **Trajaneum** (7), a Corinthian temple built for the emperor Trajan and completed *c*. AD 125 by his successor, Hadrian, who was also worshipped here. The Trajaneum is of the type known as hexastyle peripteral, with six columns at each end; in addition it has nine columns along its sides and a pair of columns *in antis* in its front porch.

The temple stands in the centre of a vast *temenos*, or sacred enclosure, bordered on its sides and rear by towering colonnades; the columns to the rear stand on top of a 5m-high (16 ft) wall. It was built there partly to buttress the rising rock-face of the acropolis and also so that this colonnade would be visible from the theatre terrace below. The re-erected columns are crowned by several varieties of palm-leaf capitals, which are late variants of the Pergamene capital.

The principal temple of Hellenistic Pergamum was the **Temple of Athena Polias** (8), the protectress of the city, the ruins of which are directly above the theatre. This is the oldest extant temple at Pergamum, dating from the beginning of the third century BC, and was probably built by Philetaerus. It is one of the very rare Doric temples in Asia Minor, a *peripteros* with six columns on its ends and ten along its flanks, with two columns *in antis* in both its front and rear porches. The use of the Doric order here is probably due to the influence of the Parthenon, which Philetaerus would have used as an archetype for the principal temple of his

30

The Trajaneum.

new capital, the Athens of Asia Minor.

The temple stood at the open front end of a **temenos** (9) nearly as large as that of the Trajaneum, bordered on the other three sides by two-storeyed stoas, with the lower storey in the Doric order and the upper in the Ionic. The temenos was adorned with bronze statues on marble bases, most of them commemorating the great victory that Attalus I won over the Gauls in 230 BC. A number of these bronze statues were later copied in marble, the most famous being the 'Dying Gaul', now in the Capitoline Museum in Rome.

Just beyond the east end of the north stoa of Athena's temenos are the remains of the famous **library** (10), which was built by Eumenes II. According to ancient sources, some 200,000 scrolls were kept here, a collection surpassed only by the library in Alexandria. After that library burnt in 41 BC, Antony looted the Pergamene library to make up the loss to Cleopatra.

The reading-room of the library was the largest of the four extant sections; one can still see there the wall-sockets that supported the shelves where the scroll collection was kept. Also visible is a pedestal that once supported a large statue of Athena, patron of learning; this was 3.5 m (11½ ft) in height and stood on a 3 m (9¾ ft) pedestal, giving one some idea of the grand dimensions of the reading-room. The statue of Athena, which is now preserved in the Berlin Museum, is a marble copy in reduced size of the colossal

31

chryselephantine (gold-and-ivory) cult-figure of Athena Parthenos that stood in the cella of the Parthenon. This statue, which dates from the first half of the second century BC, is clear evidence that the Attalids modelled their city on Athens.

Just to the south of Athena's sanctuary are the remains of a **Hellenistic stoa** (11), and south of that is the site of the great **Altar of Zeus** (12), of which only the stepped platform remains. The altar was built by Eumenes II soon after his victory over the Gauls in 190 BC, and commemorates both his own triumph and the earlier one of Attalus I.

The altar was set on a tiered podium surmounted by an Ionic stoa with two projecting wings, the latter flanking a broad flight of steps that led up to the long open side of the shrine. The Ionic stoa stood on top of a sculptured frieze, 2.3 m (7½ ft) high and 120 m (394 ft) in length, which extended all the way around the podium and up the front staircase. The theme of the frieze was the Gigantomachy, the mythical battle between the Olympian gods and the ancient Giants, symbolizing the triumphs of the Pergamene kingdom over the Gauls, and at the same time glorifying the heroic role of

The site of the Altar of Zeus.

the Attalids as the saviours of Hellenic civilization in its struggle against barbarism. The walls that surrounded the altar on three sides were also decorated with reliefs depicting the life of Telephos, son of Heracles, the mythical founder of the city.

The reconstructed Altar of Zeus.

The Altar of Zeus was destroyed during the Byzantine period and its architectural elements and reliefs used to repair the defence wall of the acropolis, where they were recovered when Pergamum was excavated in 1871 by the German engineer Carl Humann. These fragments were used in the reconstruction of the altar which is in the Berlin Museum.

North of the altar's temenos there are the remains of a line of shops dating from the Hellenistic period, and to its south is a Doric **agora** (13) dating to the third century BC. At the northwestern side of this market square are the remains of the **agora temple** (14), built in the second century BC and probably dedicated to either Zeus or Hermes; this was also in the Doric order, but it included Ionic elements. One of the objects found by the archaeologists excavating this agora was the superb marble head of Alexander (illustrated on p. 5) now in the Istanbul Archaeological Museum. This is a second-century BC copy of the original by the Greek sculptor Lysippus, who made a number of statues of Alexander from life.

The northwestern end of the agora opens up onto the **theatre terrace** (15), a long and narrow shelf that stretches for nearly 250 m (275 yd) to the north below the auditorium of the theatre. The terrace was bordered on its western side by a Doric stoa, which was one storey high on its inner side and three on the outside, where it was supported by a retaining wall. In places, this wall was five storeys high because of the very steep slope of the hillside. The view from the terrace, looking out over the lands that belonged to Pergamum when it first became an independent state, is stupendous.

At the northern end of the terrace a flight of 25 steps leads up to the remains of a small but elegant Ionic **Temple of Dionysus** (16), god of the theatre. The temple was originally erected in the first half of the second century BC, but the present remains date from the reign of Caracalla (AD 211–17), who was worshipped there during his reign as the 'new Dionysus'. It is a prostyle temple having external columns in front of its porch, and opens onto a portico; it has four columns in front and two along the frontal sides.

The **theatre** (17) is one of the most impressive monuments in Asia Minor that date from the Hellenistic age. It was originally constructed in the third century BC, then rebuilt by Eumenes II, and altered once again in Roman times. The *cavea*, or auditorium, forms part of the natural contour of the steeply sloping west face of the acropolis rock. (At the top of this rock the principal sanctuaries of the upper city, the Trajaneum and the Temple of Athena, would once have been dramatic landmarks visible from the plain below.) The auditorium is exceptionally steep, with 80 rows of seats ascending the slope through an elevation of 36 m (111 ft), and because of the lie of the land it forms an angle much more acute than in typical Greek or Roman theatres. The seats are arranged in three tiers separated by broad horizontal passages called *diazomata*, with narrow stairways dividing these into six or seven *cunei*, or sectors. Altogether there were seats for 10,000 spectators, with the king's marble box (still in place) just above the centre of the front row. The orchestra extends out onto the theatre terrace, where in Hellenistic times a wooden *skene*, or stage-building, was erected on the day of a performance and dismantled immediately afterwards, so as not to spoil the superb natural view.

An ancient road with ruts of wagon-wheels leads down from the upper agora to the middle city. This section represents an expansion of the *polis* by Eumenes II, who extended the line of fortifications down from the citadel to enclose the new quarter. On the way down one passes on the left an archaeological zone that was first explored in 1973. The most remarkable monument excavated here is the marble hall of a gymnasium-baths complex, with a heroum dedicated *c*. 70 BC to a prominent Pergamene who was probably the philanthropist identified by an inscription as Diodorus Pasparos.

The surviving monuments in the middle city include the lower agora; three gymnasia; four temples; two monumental public fountains; and a number of other structures, including altars, stoas, propylaea, and a **curved stairway** (1).

The oldest of the temples is the **Temple of Demeter** (2), constructed by Philetaerus and his brother Eumenes in memory of their mother Boa, and later enlarged by Apollonia, wife of Attalus I. It is of the type called *templum-in-antis*, that is, with columns only between its *antae*, in this case a pair of columns forming the entrance. This interesting structure combines all the Greek architectural orders and their variants; its columns were Doric; their capitals were Pergamene, and Ionic and Corinthian elements were added later, in the Roman period. The Pergamene capitals are classic examples of their type.

The second of the four temples is a short distance to the east of Demeter's temenos above the uppermost of the gymnasia, all three of which date from the second half of the third century BC, at the latest. This is the **Temple of Hera Basileia** (3), the queen of the gods, a four-columned Doric prostyle temple, which was probably erected by Attalus II.

Between the temenos of Hera and that of Demeter the archaeologists have also unearthed a **Temple of Asclepius** (4), the healing-god, whose main sanctuary is in the lower city. In its present form this is a six-columned Ionic prostyle temple and dates from the latter half of the second century BC. But recent studies have revealed that when the temple was first erected in the third century BC it was in the Doric order, and was later restored in the Ionic order when that style was made popular by Hermogenes.

Plan of the middle
city.
1. curved stairway;
2. Temple of
Demeter; 3. Temple
of Hera Basileia
4. Temple of
Asclepius;
5. gymnasium temple;
6. lower gymnasium;
7. street; 8. House of
the Consul Attalus.

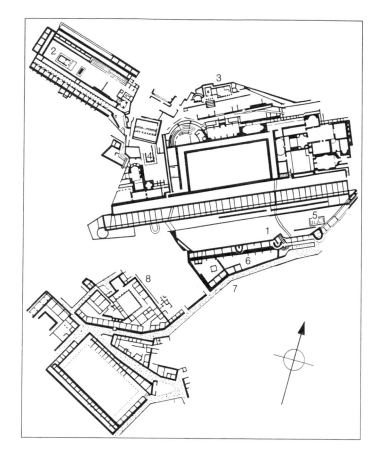

The fourth sanctuary is the **gymnasium temple** (5). This is
a four-columned prostyle temple in the Corinthian order,
erected in the second half of the second century BC. It was
originally dedicated to Hermes and Heracles, the patron
deities of athletes, but in the Imperial Roman era it was also
a shrine of the deified Emperor.

The residential quarter of the middle city was just above
the **lower gymnasium** (6), where a **street** (7) and a complex
of houses and shops from the Hellenistic period have been
excavated by the German archaeologists. One of these is
the **House of the Consul Attalus** (8), a peristyle structure
built in the Hellenistic era and modified in Roman times.

The ancient road from the acropolis goes all the way
down to the base of the mountain on its southern side, where

36

one leaves the Hellenistic city through the south gate. This interesting and complicated portal was erected by Eumenes II when he extended the fortifications of Pergamum to enclose the middle city.

The main road back into Bergama from the south gate passes the largest monument surviving from ancient Pergamum, the edifice known in Turkish as Kízíl Avlu, the Red Courtyard. This gigantic structure consists of two tower-like circular buildings and the northern end of an enormous courtyard, which measures 100 × 200 m (328 × 656 ft). Much of this courtyard is covered by modern houses above it. The Selinus River (Bergama Çayi) flows diagonally beneath it in a large tunnel of Roman construction. The whole complex dates from the reign of Hadrian. The statues still standing in its courtyard indicate that it was probably a sanctuary of the Egyptian deities Isis, Serapis and Harpocrates. The worship of these deities, particularly that of Serapis, became very popular in the Imperial Roman period, when Egyptian merchants settled in the larger cities of Asia Minor and introduced the Greeks and Romans to their cults. Around AD 400 the central hall of the structure was converted into a church and dedicated to St. John the Theologian.

THE TEMPLE OF SERAPIS

The most important site by far remaining from the lower city of Pergamum is the Asclepieum, in the southwestern quarter of Bergama. It is approached via a signposted road turning off to the right from the main avenue of the modern town. From the car-park at the end of the turn-off one approaches the Asclepieum along a splendid **colonnaded way** (1), known in Roman times as the Via Tecta. This was a bazaar street that catered to the pilgrims and patients who came to the Asclepieum, one of the most famous shrines and therapeutic centres in the classical world.

The cult of Asclepius, the god of healing, seems to have spread here from Epidaurus early in the fourth century BC, when the first sanctuary of his cult was built on this site. Sanctuaries of Asclepius usually surrounded a sacred spring whose waters were believed to have healing powers. In addition to the mystical rites of the cult they provided sound medical treatment, including the interpretation of dreams in

THE ASCLEPIEUM

Plan of the Asclepieum.
1. colonnaded way;
2. forecourt;
3. propylon;
4. Temple of Zeus
Asclepius; 5. hospital;
6. library; 7. theatre;
8. source of the
sacred spring;
9. Roman fountain;
10. three small
temples.

cases of psychological complaints.

The Pergamene Asclepieum was extended and rebuilt at various times in the Hellenistic and Roman periods; most of the ruins one sees here today date from the first half of the second century AD, when the shrine reached the height of its popularity, surpassing Epidaurus as the principal therapeutic centre in the Graeco-Roman world. Galen, the most renowned physician in the Roman era, was born in Pergamum in AD 129 and received his first training in medicine at the Pergamene Asclepieum.

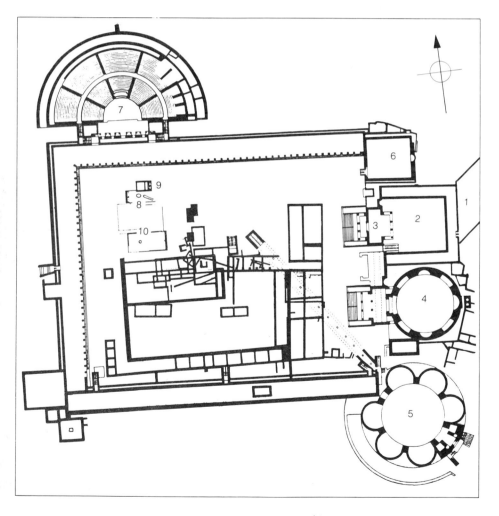

One enters the Asclepieum through what was once the propylon, the **forecourt** (2) of which formed the western end of the Via Tecta. This dates from the reign of Antoninus Pius (AD 138–61). The **propylon** (3) led into the main area of the shrine, a vast courtyard measuring 110 × 130 m (360 × 430 ft). This was originally in the Ionic order, but after an earthquake in AD 178 the columns at the east end of the north stoa were given Corinthian capitals. The two large buildings on the left inside the gateway were the principal edifices of the shrine; the one just beside the gateway was the **Temple of Zeus-Asclepius** (4), and the one beyond that, at the southeast corner of the courtyard, was the main **hospital** (5), from which a vaulted tunnel leads to the centre of the courtyard. The temple, which dates from *c*. AD 150, is a somewhat larger than half-size copy of the Pantheon at Rome. The structure at the northeast corner of the courtyard was the **library** (6), where there was also a shrine of the deified Emperor.

Outside the western end of the north stoa is the handsome Roman **theatre** (7), which has a seating capacity of approximately 3,500. The patients and their visitors were enter-

A Corinthian column from the north colonnade of the Asclepieum.

Hellenistic stoa at the west end of the Asclepieum, with the theatre behind.

tained here by performances of drama and music. Gladiatorial combats and mock naval battles were staged in the amphitheatre, whose remains can still be seen about a kilometre to the northwest of the shrine.

Directly in front of the theatre, near the northwest corner of the courtyard, a crack in the rock marks the **source of the sacred spring** (8) that was the ancient core of this shrine. Just to its north there is a **Roman fountain** (9) where the patients drank from this spring and bathed themselves in its healing waters, which were probably radioactive. Just to the south of the spring, rectangular cuttings in the rock mark the location of **three small temples** (10) known to have been located within the shrine.

The Bergama Museum, which is on the west side of the main avenue of the town, has antiquities from both the Asclepieum and the Hellenistic city on the acropolis, as well as from the cities of ancient Aeolia.

Sculptural decoration from the Asclepieum.

NORTHERN IONIA

The ancient boundary between Aeolis and Ionia was the River Hermus, known in Turkish as the Gediz Çayí. This river rises in the mountains of Phrygia and reaches the Aegean out on the northern arm of the Gulf of Smyrna, Turkish Izmir. Ionia extended from there down to the Poseidoneium, a sanctuary of the sea-god on the promontory below Didyma, which looked south to the Carian shore.

The original members of the Ionian League, the Dodeca-polis, included the islands of Chios and Samos and ten cities on the mainland opposite them: Phocaea, Clazomenae, Erythrae, Teos, Lebedus, Colophon, Ephesus, Priene, Myus and Miletus. Their central shrine and meeting-place, the Panionium, was on the mainland just north of Cape Mycale, the promontory opposite Samos. The people of the twelve cities gathered there from the early archaic period onwards, excluding all outsiders from their meetings, even the citizens of other Ionian towns that were not members of the Dodecapolis. Smyrna, which was originally Aeolian, was taken over by Ionians from Colophon soon after its founda-tion; nevertheless, the city was not made a member of the Ionian League until the early third century BC, when the Dodecapolis was long past the days of its glory.

The golden age of Ionia began in the seventh century BC, early in the archaic period, by which time the Greek cities on the Aegean coast of Asia Minor had already established colonies all over the Mediterranean, as well as along the Dardanelles, the Sea of Marmara, the Bosphorus and the Black Sea. The renaissance of Greek culture in Ionia began with Homer, who is believed to have flourished in the second half of the eighth century BC. During the three centuries that followed, Ionia produced a succession of immortals in the intellectual pantheon of Greece: Lesbos gave birth to the poets Alcaeus and Sappho; Teos to the poet Anacreon; Colophon to the poets Mimnermus and Xenophanes, who won even greater fame as a philosopher; Samos to the philosopher and mathematician Pythagoras, and the astronomer Aristarchus; Clazomenae to the philosopher

The northern Ionian shore.

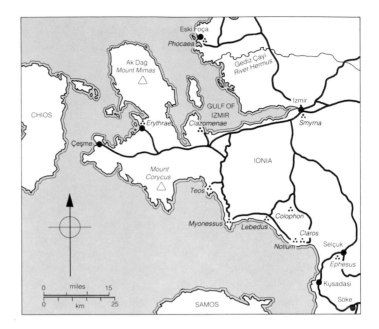

Anaxagoras; Ephesus to the philosopher Heracleitus; Miletus to the philosophers of nature Thales, Anaximander and Anaximines, the geographer Hecataeus, and the city-planner Hippodamus; and Chios to the physician Hippocrates; to name only those who won enduring fame. But then one must also include the Samians Rhoecus and Theodorus, the first architects in the world to be identified by name.

The sites of the northern Ionian cities can easily be seen using Izmir as a base, whereas Ephesus and the other cities of the Dodecapolis to its south can be most conveniently reached from either Selçuk or Kuşadasí. All but one of the northern sites are on or close to the coast around the enormous and hydra-headed peninsula that forms the southern arm of the Gulf of Izmir. The single exception is Phocaea, which is on the outer end of the peninsula that encloses the gulf to the north, facing Mount Mimas at the other side of the great Ionian fiord.

PHOCAEA (ESKI FOÇA)

Despite their brilliant past, there is little left to be seen of most of the northern Ionian cities, although their sites are beautiful and evocative. The most outstanding site is that of Phocaea, now known as Eski Foça, which is on a magnificent bay reached by a road from the coastal highway north of Izmir, the whole length of the drive amounting to about 65 km (40 miles). The only monument in Eski Foça is a ruined Genoese fortress dating from the late Byzantine period, when the town was known as Foglia Vecchia. Absolutely nothing is left of the ancient Ionian city, whose mariners rivalled those of Miletus in their colonizing ventures, and whose valour was renowned throughout Greece.

Modern Izmir, the third largest metropolis in Turkey after Istanbul and Ankara, spreads around the whole inner end of the great gulf that since antiquity has been the maritime gateway to western Anatolia. Izmir itself, known to the Greeks as Smyrna, is by far the oldest city on the Aegean coast and rivals even Troy in its antiquity.

The site of the most ancient remnant of Smyrna is at Bayraklí, now an industrial suburb of Izmir at the inner end of the gulf. The first archaeological excavations at Bayraklí were made in 1948–51 by John Cook and Ekrem Akurgal, who established that this was the original site of ancient Smyrna. The excavations indicate that the site was inhabited in the first half of the third millennium BC, the oldest strata of the settlement being thus contemporary with Troy I and II. Virtually nothing is known of the pre-Hellenic inhabitants of Smyrna, except that they may have been the indigenous Anatolian people whom the Greeks called Lelegians.

Smyrna was first settled by Hellenic people at the beginning of the first millennium BC, undoubtedly in the Aeolian migration, as evidenced by the discovery at Bayraklí of large quantities of pottery shards of that era. The excavations also unearthed houses dating from the ninth to the seventh century BC, as well as an archaic Temple of Athena, which ranks with the temple at Neandria among the earliest extant Greek sanctuaries in Asia Minor.

The original Temple of Athena was built c. 640 BC, but this was destroyed c. 600 BC when Smyrna was sacked by the Lydians under King Alyattes. The people of Smyrna then built another temple, but this too was soon destroyed, demolished by the Persians under Harpagus the Mede in 545 BC. The excavations at Bayraklí indicate that by 500 BC the Temple of Athena had been restored, but the city itself never recovered its former stature. During the classical period Smyrna was little more than a collection of villages, abandoned altogether at the beginning of the Hellenistic period when the city was re-built on a new site on Mount Pagus, the flat-topped hill that rises above the present port-quarter of Izmir.

The re-founding of Smyrna was attributed to Alexander the Great, but construction on the new site was not begun until more than two decades after his death. The city flourished during the Hellenistic and Roman eras, when its population grew to more than 100,000. During that time numerous splendid public buildings were erected, which, set against the natural beauty of their position, elicited praise from writers throughout antiquity.

The most prominent ancient monument in Izmir is the ruined fortress that crowns Kadifekale, the Velvet Castle, which was the acropolis of the Hellenistic city. The ruins that one sees there today are the remains of the citadel, from which two parallel lines of defence walls extended down to the port to enclose the lower city. The lower walls have vanished, and all that survives are the fortifications on Kadifekale. The foundations and perhaps a few of the lower courses were built some time after 295 BC; the remainder date from successive reconstructions by the Romans, Byzantines and Ottoman Turks.

The only ancient monument that has survived in the lower town is the agora, which is midway between Mount Pagus and the port. This was originally built in the mid-second century AD, but was destroyed in the earthquake of AD 178 that levelled most of the city. The agora was rebuilt soon afterwards in its present form by the empress Faustina II, wife of Marcus Aurelius (AD 161–80). This structure consisted of a central courtyard, 120 × 80 m (394 × 262 ft), surrounded by Corinthian stoas, of which only those on the north and west sides have been excavated. Beneath the north stoa there is a splendid vaulted basement, above which there was a line of shops that opened out onto a Roman market street. Some of the sculptures that once adorned the agora are now in the new Izmir Archaeological Museum; the most notable of these are statues of Poseidon and Demeter, the principal figures in a beautiful and well-preserved group dating from the Imperial Roman era. These statues symbolized the two sources of ancient Smyrna's wealth — its seaborne commerce and its agriculture — for Poseidon was god of the sea and Demeter goddess of the harvest.

The other northern Ionian sites are either due west of Izmir along the gulf or south across the base of the great peninsula that points out to Chios. Clazomenae is 34 km (21 miles) away, nearly halfway out along the northern shore of the peninsula, and Erythrae is at its western end 81 km (50 miles) away, just opposite Chios. Teos is farthest out on the southern shore of the peninsula, 52 km (32 miles) from Izmir, facing west across a bay towards Mount Corycus. To its east are Myonessus, Lebedus, Colophon, Claros and Notium. Myonessus, a tiny sea-girt town, and Claros, site of a famous oracle of Apollo, were not members of the Dodecapolis, nor was Notium, which in fact was Aeolian in foundation. But they all belonged to the ancient Ionian world, and were part of the scenery described in one of the most lyrical passages of the *Homeric Hymns*:

> Chios, brightest of all the isles that lie in the sea, and craggy Mimas and the heights of Corycus and gleaming Claros and the sheer hill of Aesagea ...

The most famous monument that has survived among the ruins of northern Ionia is the Temple of Dionysus at Teos. Its site is one of the most romantic in Asia Minor, with the mottled ruins of the temple embowered in an olive grove beside the Aegean. The temple was built in the early or middle second century BC by Hermogenes, and was considered by Vitruvius to be the archetypal temple of the Ionic order. This was the largest temple to Dionysus ever erected in the ancient world, with a stylobate measuring 18.5 × 35 m (61 × 115 ft). The temple was hexastyle peripteral, having six columns to front and rear, and eleven along the sides with a pair of columns *in antis* in both the front and back porches.

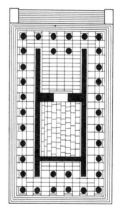

Plan of the Temple of Dionysus, Teos.

EPHESUS

The main highway south from Izmir leads to Selçuk, which is 94 km (59 miles) away, the base for most travellers who come to visit Ephesus by land. Those travelling by sea usually arrive at Kuşadasí, from where a drive of 19 km (12 miles) across the delta of the River Cayster brings one to Selçuk. The remains of the medieval city, which was known as Ayasuluk, are on the hill just above Selçuk, whereas the ancient ruins are centred about 2 km (1¼ miles) farther to the southwest, in the valley between Panayir Dağí and Bülbül Dağí, the eminences that were known to the Greeks as mounts Pion and Coressus.

The site of Ephesus has changed several times during the course of its long history. The local topography has changed as well, for in antiquity the sea came in as far as the foot of the Ayasuluk hill, whereas now the coast is some 6½ km (4 miles) away, the intervening countryside created by silt carried down to the coast by the Cayster. The original Ionian settlement, which was probably colonized no later than the tenth century BC, was on the seashore below the northern slopes of mounts Pion and Coressus.

When the Ionians arrived they found that the indigenous people worshipped an ancient Anatolian fertility goddess named Cybele, and so they assimilated her into the Greek pantheon by combining her cult with that of the Greek fertility goddess Artemis, the twin sister of Apollo. The Ephesians built their first temple of Artemis on the same site as the original shrine of Cybele, at the foot of the Ayasuluk hill. The colossal edifice that succeeded it, the archaic Artemisium, was erected in the mid-sixth century BC.

During the reign of Croesus, the last and greatest of the Lydian kings, the Ephesians were forced to leave their strongly fortified port and move inland to a new site around the Artemisium. Then early in the fourth century BC the site of Ephesus was changed once again, when, after the death of Alexander, Lysimachus re-established it on what was then the coast, where the ruins of the Graeco-Roman city are to be seen today.

(*Opposite*) The Library of Celsus.

47

THE ARTEMISIUM

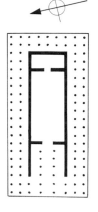

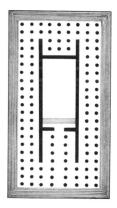

Plan of the archaic Artemisium (*top*) and the later Artemisium (*bottom*).

Façade capital from the archaic Artemisium.

The site of the **Artemisum** (1) is just below the Ayasuluk hill to the south, on the right side of the road leading out to the main archaeological site. The earliest shrine of Artemis discovered on this site is an altar dated to *c*. 700 BC. This would have enshrined the sacred cult-objects of Cybele-Artemis, including her xoanon. During the century that followed the Ephesians enclosed this altar in a naiskos, which was rebuilt on a larger scale *c*. 600 BC

The archaic Artemisium was begun *c*. 560 BC, probably just after the completion of the Heraeum on Samos. The Cretan Chersiphron was the chief architect, assisted by his son Metagenes and also by Theodorus of Samos, who brought to the project all of the vast experience he must have gained in the design and construction of the Samian Heraeum, which, like the Artemisium, was built on an immense platform that had to be filled in on marshy ground.

The first temple to be constructed entirely of marble, the archaic Artemisium was also one of the two largest edifices ever built in the Greek world, the other being its Hellenistic successor, the so-called 'later Artemisium', which was erected on the same foundations and designed along virtually the same lines. The archaic Artemisium is sometimes called the 'Croesus Temple', because King Croesus of Lydia was its principal benefactor.

The archaic Artemisium stood for two centuries, surviving undamaged through most of the Persian occupation of Asia Minor. But then in 356 BC it was burned down by a madman named Herostratus, who thus sought to immortalize his name. The Ephesians immediately set out to rebuild the temple, a project that is said to have taken 120 years. The original architects of the 'later Artemisum' were Paeonius and Demetrius, both of Ephesus, the latter identified as a 'slave of Artemis'.

The Artemisium was still being built in 334 BC when Alexander the Great passed through Ephesus, early in his invasion of Asia. When he saw the partially rebuilt ruins of the temple, Alexander offered to cover the expenses for its complete reconstruction, but the Ephesians politely declined, saying that it was not fitting for one god to make a dedication to another deity. Nevertheless, Alexander undoubtedly contributed generously to the rebuilding of the Artemisium, since he appointed an architect to supervise the

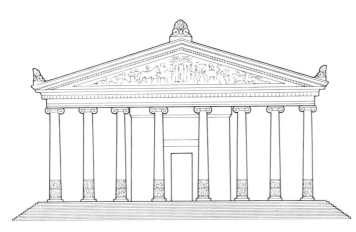

A restoration of the west front of the later Artemisium.

Carved column drum from the later Artemisium, showing Alcestis (?) between Death and Hermes.

project, a man whose name is given variously as Cheiro-crates or Deinocrates. The Hellenistic Artemisium was built on the same colossal scale as its archaic predecessor, and its even more magnificent sculptural decoration caused it to be ranked among the Seven Wonders of the Ancient World, along with the Mausoleum at Halicarnassus.

The Hellenistic Artemisium stood on a 13-stepped *crepidoma*, or stepped platform, 2.68 m (8¾ ft) in height with a stylobate that measured 55.1 × 115 m (170 × 377 ft), which was three times as great as that of the Parthenon. A highly unusual feature of the Artemisium was that it did not face east, as was customary, but west, for that was the orientation of the ancient altar of Artemis-Cybele, which was preserved at the exact centre of the temple's cella, enclosed in its naiskos. It was a dipteral temple, that is, surrounded by a covered, double colonnade, though there were three rows of columns at the front end. The columns, 111 in all, were 17.65 m (58 ft) tall and those in the front rows were carved with reliefs, the *columnae caelatea*, one of whose sculptors was reputed to be Scopas. These reliefs were probably on the lower drums of the columns at the west front of the temple.

THE CITY

The main entrance to the archaeological site is a kilometre past the Artemisium. Just inside the entrance on the left one comes to the **Gymnasium of Vedius** (2), erected in AD 150 by a wealthy Ephesian named Publius Vedius Antonius, who dedicated it to Artemis and the emperor Antoninus Pius. This was a combined gymnasium and public baths; it had a complex of 16 rooms of various sizes on the west side of the building, and on the east, a large colonnaded courtyard, the *palaestra*, where the athletes exercised. The propylon of the palaestra is on its southern side; at the centre of its west colonnade there is a large room that may have been reserved for the Emperor. This is the best-preserved of the eight gymnasium-baths complexes that have been unearthed in Ephesus.

Just beyond the gymnasium is the Roman **stadium** (3), which was erected in the reign of Nero (AD 54–68) and was altered in the third or fourth century AD. The tiers of seats on the south side of the stadium were hollowed out of the lower slopes of Mount Pion, whereas those on the north were supported on a vaulted substructure. The principal remnant

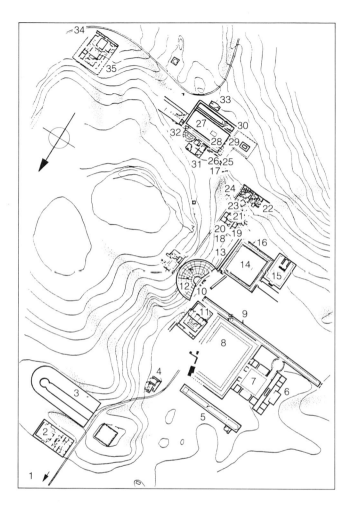

City plan of Ephesus.
1. Artemisium;
2. Gymnasium of Vedius; 3. stadium;
4. Palace of the Proconsul of Asia;
5. financial exchange;
6. gymnasium-baths complex; 7. harbour gymnasium;
8. Portico Verulanus;
9. Arcadiane;
10. fountain;
11. theatre gymnasium;
12. theatre;
13. Marble Way;
14. commercial agora; 15. Temple of Serapis; 16. Library of Celsus; 17. the Embolos; 18. latrines; 19. brothel; 20. Baths of Scholastica; 21. Temple of Hadrian; 22. residential quarter; 23. Nymphaeum of Trajan; 24. Gate of Heracles; 25. Hydreion; 26. Memmius Monument; 27. state agora; 28. Pollio Fountain; 29. Temple of Domitian; 30. Inscription Gallery; 31. prytaneum; 32. odeum; 33. fountain; 34. Magnesia Gate; 35. east gymnasium.

of the stadium is its great round-arched entrance and the adjacent part of the façade.

Some 250 m (270 yd) beyond the stadium, on the right, one comes to a complex known until recent years as the Byzantine Baths. This has now been identified as the **Palace of the Proconsul of Asia** (4), the governor of the province, and probably dates from the reign of Diocletian.

Just beyond the Proconsul's Palace a side path to the right leads west towards the ancient harbour, which was about a kilometre distant. This runs to a long and extremely narrow building, measuring 260 × 30 m (680 × 98 ft), divided by two rows of columns into a nave and side aisles, with apse-shaped *exedrae* at either end. This is believed to have been originally a **financial exchange** (5), constructed during the first half of the second century AD, when Ephesus was the banking centre for all of Asia Minor. At the beginning of the fourth century the Ephesian Christians converted this into a church dedicated to the Virgin Mary, which became the first cathedral of Ephesus.

The area just to the south of the church is a vast field of ruins that was originally, but erroneously, known as the Baths of Constantius (AD 337–61). Now it has been identified as a **gymnasium-baths complex** (6), dating from the reign of Domitian (AD 81–96), faced in marble during Hadrian's reign by Claudius Verulanus, chief priest of Asia. The baths were themselves only a small part of the most enormous complex of public buildings in Ephesus. This labyrinthian edifice covered an area of 500 × 300 m (550 × 330 yd) and comprised, besides the baths themselves, the **harbour gymnasium** (7) and an enormous palaestra called the **Portico Verulanus** (8), which alone takes up an area of 200 × 200 m (220 × 220 yd) on each side, making it far larger than any other public building in the city.

Beyond the baths complex to the south one comes to the **Arcadiane** (9), a remarkably well-preserved and impressive colonnaded avenue leading from the former harbour to the theatre, a distance of some 600 m (650 yd). This promenade takes its name from the emperor Arcadius (AD 395–408), during whose reign it was given its present form. Double colonnades flanked covered porticoes with mosaic pavements on both sides; monumental gateways stood at each end; and 100 street-lamps in two rows illuminated the avenue in the evening.

At the western end of the Arcadiane, set into the northwest corner by the theatre terrace wall, is a **Hellenistic fountain** (10) with two Ionic columns that open onto the courtyard. A short distance to the north of the fountain, facing the harbour baths, is the **theatre gymnasium** (11), which dates from the second century AD.

The focal point of Ephesus is the splendid and well-restored **theatre** (12), which seated 24,000, and was the largest in Asia Minor. It dates from early in the Hellenistic period, with extensive additions and reconstructions in the Roman era. The horseshoe-shaped auditorium extends

through an angle of 220 degrees, with a diameter of 150 m (492 ft), its uppermost tier 30 m (98 ft) above the orchestra, its middle sector still surmounted by an arcade. Originally, the actors in the Greek theatre performed alongside the chorus in the orchestra; later, in the Hellenistic period, they acted on a stage, the proscenium, which was erected in front of the skene, or stage-building. The core of the Hellenistic skene remains in the ruin of the monumental Roman stage-building. This ornate structure originally had three storeys; in front of it was the broad stage, raised high above the level of the orchestra on three rows of Doric columns, the stumps of which still remain in place.

The theatre at Ephesus was also the focal point of the annual midsummer festival celebrating the birth of Artemis. In this ritual the sacred image of the goddess was taken from

View of the theatre from the Arcadiane.

53

the Artemisium and carried in procession around the city before its return to the temple. The theatre was the scene of the mass meeting of the Ephesians described in *Acts of the Apostles*, where the silversmiths protested against the missionary activities of St. Paul, crying out *en masse*, 'Great is the goddess Artemis of the Ephesians.'

Turning left after leaving the theatre, one steps out onto the main street of ancient Ephesus. This is generally known as the **Marble Way** (13). The section just to the south of the theatre was paved in marble in the fifth century AD by a wealthy Ephesian named Eutropius. It created a thoroughfare that was reserved for wheeled vehicles; pedestrians used the raised pavements that flanked the avenue.

A short stroll along the Marble Way brings one to the eastern end of the main **commercial agora** (14), a vast square area that stretches off to the west, ringed with the stumps of the columns that once formed its peripheral colonnade, about 100 m (325 ft) along each side. This agora was originally built in the Ionic order during the Hellenistic period. The double Doric colonnade in two storeys that forms its eastern side was erected during the reign of Nero, whereas the gateway near the southeast corner, a triple portal, is dated by an inscription to the year 4–3 BC.

A large square off the southwest corner of the agora was once the temenos of the **Temple of Serapis** (15), an Egyptian god; an inscription records that it was also dedicated to the deified Caracalla. This temple is believed to have been erected during the second half of the second century AD by Egyptian merchants who were living in Ephesus. In the early Byzantine period it was converted into a church, whose baptistry is in the east end of the building.

Just beyond the Temple of Serapis, to the right of the Marble Way at its far end, one comes to the **Library of Celsus** (16), a unique Corinthian structure which has now been splendidly restored. Inscriptions in both Greek and Latin record that it was founded in AD 110 by the consul Gaius Julius Aquila as a funerary monument for his father, Gaius Celsus Polemaenus, who had been a Roman senator and Proconsul of Asia. It stands at the western end of a marble courtyard, its main door approached by a flight of nine steps, once flanked by two statues of Celsus. The impressive, reconstructed façade of the library has as its principal structures four pairs of columns supporting beams on each of its two storeys. The three entrances are flanked by four niches which contain statues personifying the virtues of Celsus; copies of these statues now replace the originals. Inside the library were two towering chambers, with a two-tiered gallery that contained the rectangular niches in which some 12,000 books were stored. The semicircular niche in the main floor facing the central portal probably contained a statue of Athena.

The Marble Way ends at a junction just past the agora and the library. From there another street, named the **Embolos** (17), or Colonnaded Way, runs up through the valley between mounts Pion and Coressus. The principal thoroughfare of Ephesus, the Embolos was lined with arcaded shops, monumental fountains, honorific statues and an imperial temple. (The Embolos is also known as Curetes Street, after an order of Ephesian priests.)

At the lower end of the Embolos, just opposite the forecourt of the library and on the left side of the avenue, extended one of its many colonnades. At the far end of the colonnade, just before the first street on the left, were the public **latrines** (18), which apparently were next to a **brothel** (19). This is one of the best-preserved examples of a Roman public lavatory, with many of the toilet seats still intact, along with the channel that conducted the water in which the customers cleansed themselves. The group of buildings across the side street from the latrines are the **Baths of Scholastica** (20), the largest in Ephesus. The baths were lavishly rebuilt later in the fourth century AD by a Christian woman called Scholastica.

The baths stand behind the most beautiful edifice in Ephesus, the little Corinthian **Temple of Hadrian** (21), whose reconstructed porch opens directly onto the Embolos. The temple façade consists of two pairs of columns which frame the arched entrance to the porch; the architrave is decorated with an interesting relief in which the central figure, forming the keystone of the arch, is a bust of Tyche, the goddess of fortune and protectress of the city. This is one of the earliest examples of an arch supported on columns rather than piers, an amalgamation of Greek and Roman architectural forms that led directly into Romanesque architecture. The inscription above the architrave relates that the temple was built by an Ephesian named P. Quintillius in honour of the deified emperor Hadrian. The temple was

The Temple of Hadrian.

restored during the fourth century AD, when a figurative relief was added to the upper part of the porch walls, together with the lunette opposite the entrance which portrays a naked girl emerging from a foliate scroll. The figures in the relief, which are copies of the originals in the archaeological museum in Selçuk, are also from the fourth century AD, and were probably taken from some other building in Ephesus. The scenes in the relief depict the myth of the city's founding by Prince Androclus, a son of King Codrus of Athens.

On the lower slopes of Mount Coressus, opposite the Temple of Hadrian, are the latest excavations at Ephesus; these have unearthed an entire **residential quarter** (22) of the late Roman city. The inhabitants seem to have been very prosperous; the most luxurious dwellings consist of a congeries of rooms built around a peristyle court; some of the villas retain their marble and mosaic pavements, and large areas of the walls are painted with frescoes.

A short way beyond the Temple of Hadrian a side street to the left leads from the Embolos to the upper entrance of the theatre. Just beyond this intersection is the partially restored

Nymphaeum of Trajan (23). An inscription records that the fountain was built in AD 102–4 by T. Claudius Aristion, who dedicated it to the emperor Trajan (AD 98–117). The fountain contained a monumental statue of Trajan, surrounded by statues of other emperors, gods and heroes.

The Embolos continues uphill as far as the **Gate of Heracles** (24) which marked the end of the avenue for vehicles; the rest of the way was for pedestrians only. The gate is named after the two figures in relief on the western sides of its pillars — they depict Heracles wearing the skin of the Nemaean Lion, which he killed in one of his twelve labours. These pillars date from the second century AD; they originally stood elsewhere in the city and were erected here only in the fourth or fifth century.

At the upper end of Curetes Street on its left side there are the remains of two minor monuments adorned with rather attractive reliefs. The first of these is a semi-circular fountain, the **Hydreion** (25), and the second is a four-sided triumphal arch known as the **Memmius Monument** (26). The latter is identified as a funerary monument dedicated to Caicus

The Gateway of Heracles.

Memmius, whose grandfather, the Roman general Sulla, captured Ephesus in 86 BC from the forces of King Mithradates of Pontus.

Directly above these two monuments one comes to the northwest corner of the **state agora** (27), from which streets branch off along both the west and north sides of the square. A short way along the left side of the street to the west one sees a conspicuous monument framed in a reconstructed Roman arch; this is the **Pollio Fountain** (28) erected during the reign of Augustus by C. Sextillius Pollio, who at the same time constructed an aqueduct to bring water into Ephesus.

Just beyond the Pollio Fountain, on the opposite side of the street, one comes to the northeast corner of a vast temenos that surrounded a **Temple of Domitian** (29). Virtually nothing remains of the temple itself, which was relatively small compared with its colossal cult-statue of Domitian. When Domitian was assassinated in AD 96, this statue was brought down by a mob and smashed on the ground, where many of the pieces still lie; the monstrous head and an arm are kept in the Izmir Museum. The terrace that supported the temple had a very elaborate façade, of which two piers and their entablature have been erected recently, surmounted by a pair of columns decorated with reliefs representing robed figures. At the eastern end of the temple precinct there is a vaulted passageway called the **Inscription Gallery** (30); this is used to display some of the more than two thousand inscriptions that have been discovered at Ephesus, the oldest of them dating back to the seventh century BC.

The street that leads along the north side of the state agora was known as Clivus Sacer, the Sacred Way, taking its name from the procession that passed along it on the annual feast-day of Artemis. The street was also regarded as sacred because it led to the shrine of Hestia Boulea, the goddess of the hearth; this was within the **prytaneum** (31), the town hall, whose ruins are just to the left of the Clivus Sacer, near its beginning. The shrine of Hestia lay in a small room behind the main chamber of the prytaneum, and contained the sacred flame of the Ionian tribe, originally lit at the shrine of the goddess in Athens, which was kept burning for as long as her cult survived in Ephesus.

Just beyond the prytaneum the ruins of some early Byzantine houses cover the site of a small Roman temple. It was built in 27 BC for Augustus, who dedicated it to the city of Rome and the deified Julius Caesar, his adoptive father. Beyond the temple, on the same side of the street, stands an **odeum** (32) which seated about 400 people; apparently it was used as the bouleuterion, or council house, although it may also have doubled as a theatre for musical performances and ceremonial gatherings.

The opposite side of the street from the bouleuterion was formed by a stoa, which ran along the north side of the state agora. The central portion of this stoa is basilical in form; and its side aisles are defined by columns with alternating Ionic and Corinthian capitals. The Ionic columns date from the original construction in the Augustan era, whereas those of the Corinthian order were added later in the Imperial age. The basilica was probably used for meetings of the law courts and other municipal affairs.

Directly across from the bouleuterion are the ruins of a monumental **fountain** (33), built in the second century AD and restored two centuries later. This fountain and the large private baths on the northeast side of the agora were supplied with water by the Marnas aqueduct, which was built during the decade AD 4–14. An impressive section of this aqueduct can still be seen crossing a valley 5 km (3 miles) east of Ephesus along the Aydín road.

After passing the state agora one comes to the **Magnesia Gate** (34), so called because it led to the road that went to Magnesia-ad-Sipylum. Just beside the gate to the left are the remains of the **east gymnasium** (35), the baths of which would have been used by those returning to Ephesus from journeys into Asia Minor.

Those returning to Selçuk might stop at the Archaeological Museum, where the most remarkable exhibits are the two statues of Artemis Ephesia. One of these, the figure with the tower-like headdress, dates from the reign of Domitian; the second, which shows Artemis flanked by the headless figures of two tiny fawns, symbolizing her role as Mistress of Animals, has been dated to the reign of Hadrian. Both statues are adorned with extraordinary symbols of fertility. They were discovered beneath the floor of the prytaneum, where they were buried by the priests of Artemis to prevent them being destroyed, either in AD 392, when Theodosius I published his edict banning paganism, or in 401, when a Christian mob demolished the Artemisium.

SOUTHERN IONIA

There are four Ionian sites south of Ephesus: Priene, Miletus, Myus and Didyma. The first three belonged to the Dodecapolis, with Miletus and Priene ranking among the most important members of the League, and Myus the least significant. Didyma was not a city, but a religious shrine, housing an oracle of Apollo, founded under the aegis of Miletus.

As with Ephesus, the topography of this region has changed greatly since antiquity. Both areas lie in the valley of the Maeander River (in Turkish, Büyük Menderes), which over the millennia has created a vast delta along this coast. Thus, places that were once sea-ports are now marooned miles from the coast, which is one of the reasons for the decline and eventual death of some of the great cities of the Dodecapolis.

The best base for visiting the southern Ionian cities is Söke, a lively market-town some 15 km (9 miles) inland from Kuşadasí. The main highway south from Söke has a turn-off for Priene (whose site is 15 km or 9 miles from Söke), and from there one can drive south over secondary roads to Miletus and Didyma. (There is virtually nothing left of Myus, and it is hardly worth the detour.)

(*Opposite*) Medusa head from a frieze on the Temple of Apollo, Didyma.

The southern Ionian shore.

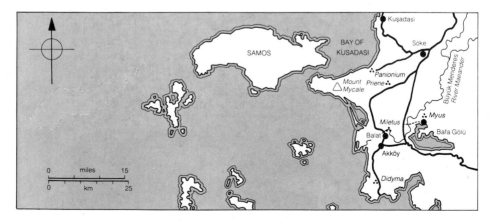

61

PRIENE

Priene is magnificently situated high above the Maeander plain on the southeastern slope of Mount Mycale, one of whose sheer rock peaks looms directly above the ancient city. Priene was always a small Greek *polis*, typical of the late classical and early Hellenistic periods, with a population probably never much more than its original 5,000.

Priene was founded in the great Ionian migration at the beginning of the first millenium BC, though its present location below Mount Mycale was established only in the mid-fourth century BC. The original site has never been found, but is probably near the ancient mouth of the Maeander, some 10 km (6 miles) to the west of the present site. Priene is by far the finest extant example of a Greek city built according to a rectangular grid-plan. It is unusual because it is the first example of the grid-plan applied to a hillside site. The city faces south, with the dramatic eastern spur of Mount Mycale at its back. The main avenues run east-west on the level, whereas the stepped side streets rise from south to north from one to another of the four tiers of the natural shelf above the Maeander plain.

Today visitors approaching the site from the pretty village below — Güllübançe, the Rosy Garden — enter the city through the northeast gate. This leads westward along one of the uppermost avenues to the **theatre** (1), whose auditorium is hollowed out of the hillside on the northern side of the street. This is one of the finest remaining theatres of the

The theatre at Priene.

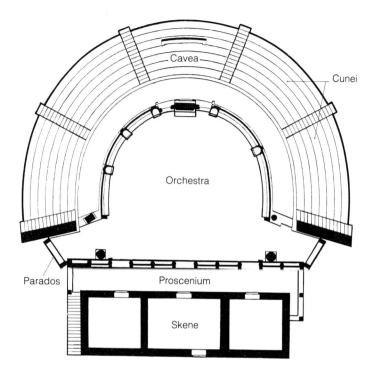

Plan of the theatre at Priene.

Marble seat in the front row of the theatre at Priene.

early Hellenistic world, and though it was somewhat modified in the Roman era it remains as archetypically Greek as the rest of Priene. Here one sees the best surviving example of the horseshoe-shaped orchestra which in Hellenistic times replaced the full circular orchestra of the classical period. The horseshoe shape developed as a result of the broadening of the stage, which began to encroach into the orchestra during this period, as the actors performed there rather than with the chorus in the orchestra. The Priene theatre seated 5,000 (indicating that people from the surrounding countryside were entertained here as well as the townspeople), and was used not only for performances of drama and other cultural activities but also for meetings of the *ecclesia*, or people's assembly, the heart of Ionian democracy.

The civic centre of Priene was just to the south of the theatre. Its principal edifices faced one another across the main eastwest avenue, with the agora and the Temple of Zeus Olympius to the south and the Sacred Stoa to the north; the northeast side of the stoa opened up to the bouleuterion

City plan of Priene.
1. theatre; 2. agora;
3. Sanctuary of Zeus
Olympius; 4. Sacred
Stoa; 5. bouleterion;
6. prytaneum;
7. upper gymnasium;
8. lower gymnasium;
9. Temple of Athena
Polias.

and the prytaneum. The **agora** (2), which dates from the third century BC, was bounded on three sides by stoas, with its north side open to the main avenue. The **Sanctuary of Zeus Olympius** (3), also erected in the third century BC, stood in a temenos, adjoining the east stoa of the agora; this was a small Ionic prostyle temple with four columns in front.

The **Sacred Stoa** (4) was erected in 130 BC directly across the avenue from the agora and the temenos of Zeus. The founder is identified by a fragmentary inscription as King Ariarthes VI of Cappadocia. This grand stoa was 160 m

The Temple of Athena Polias, Priene.

(525 ft) long and 12 m (39 ft) wide under the portico, outside which was an open promenade almost 6.5 m (21 ft) in width along the avenue, approached by a flight of six steps. The stoa had 40 Doric columns along its facade on the avenue, while 24 Ionic columns carried the wooden roof and also divided the inner hall longitudinally.

The east end of the Sacred Stoa opened to the bouleuterion, on the left, and the prytaneum, on the right, both dating from *c*. 150 BC. The **bouleuterion** (5) is one of the best-preserved and most distinctive in Asia Minor, with rectilinear tiers of seats rising from three sides of the almost square room, and the remains of an altar still standing in the centre. The adjoining **prytaneum** (6) was the meeting-place and dining-hall for the council, the executive committee of the

Plan of the bouleuterion, Priene.

boule, who were in turn responsible for the day-to-day functioning of the *polis*. As in Ephesus and all other Greek cities, the prytaneum had an inner sanctum dedicated to Hestia Boulea.

Across the street just to the north of the bouleuterion and the prytaneum are the remains of the **upper gymnasium** (7). When this was first built, in the fourth century BC, it consisted of a peristyle, surrounding a palaestra; in Roman times baths were added to the north side of the gymanasium.

There is a larger **lower gymnasium** (8) at the southernmost angle of the city, with a stadium abutting its eastern side. Both of these structures seem to have been erected *c*. 130 BC. The palaestra of this lower gymnasium was surrounded by four stoas of the Doric order; its propylon, which was also Doric, was on the west side, where it opened onto a stepped street that led up to the centre of town. The stadium was 190 m (620 ft) long, and was paralleled on its northern side by a 6-m-wide (20 ft) promenade bordered by a Doric stoa.

The **Temple of Athena Polias** (9), the oldest and most famous edifice in Priene, is two blocks west of the civic centre along the main avenue. Five columns of the temple's peripteral colonnade have been re-erected in recent years, and their mottled drums and exquisite Ionic capitals make a stirring sight against the dramatic background of the grey rock-face of the sheer acropolis behind them.

The architect was Pythius, one of the builders of the Mausoleum in Halicarnassus. According to Vitruvius this temple was described by Pythius in a lost work as the ideal

Plan of the Temple of Athena Polias, Priene.

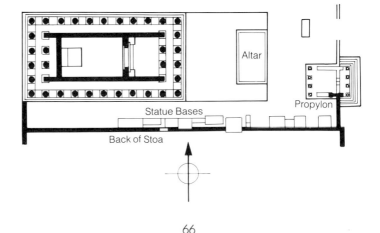

Altar

Propylon

Statue Bases

Back of Stoa

Ionic temple, and thereafter served as a model of its type. It had six columns at the front and rear and eleven on the sides, with a pair of columns *in antis* in both its front and rear porches. This was the first Ionic temple to have a rear porch, or *opisthodomus*, a feature that Pythius adopted from the Doric order; it was thenceforth included in all large Ionic temples. The temple was begun by Pythius in 340 BC and endowed in 334 BC by Alexander the Great, whose name was inscribed on one of the projecting walls of the front porch. (The inscription is now in the British Museum).

Several blocks of Prienean houses stand along the rectangular grid of streets between the civic centre and the west gate of the city. These all date from the Hellenistic period, and are among the finest and best-preserved dwellings that have survived from the classical world. One of them has been identified as a Sanctuary of Alexander the Great, perhaps commemorating his brief residence in Priene in 334 BC, when his army was besieging Miletus.

MILETUS

The back road from Priene to Miletus, a drive of some 20 km (12 miles), crosses the great delta of the Maeander, which in antiquity was a deep indentation of the sea known as the Latmian Gulf. The present site of Priene stands on what was once the long peninsula that formed the northern boundary of this gulf, ending in Cape Mycale, whereas Miletus stood on the shore of the peninsula that formed its southern arm. Now, the whole gulf has been completely silted up except for its inner end, which survives as Lake Bafa, and the once-great port of Miletus is 10 km (6 miles) from the sea on the left bank of the Maeander, which snakes its way through the marshy delta that it has created over the centuries.

The Ionians first settled at Miletus at the end of the second millennium BC. Miletus was the greatest of all the Greek cities of Asia Minor, not only in terms of its numerous overseas colonies, but also because of its contribution to Greek philosophy (the first three Greek philosophers of nature, Thales, Anaximander and Anaximenes, lived here in the last century of the archaic period), and its leadership of the revolt against Persian rule in 499–494 BC. However, the Persians finally burned it to the ground.

Miletus was destroyed again in 479 BC by Xerxes after the Persians were defeated by the Greeks at the battle of

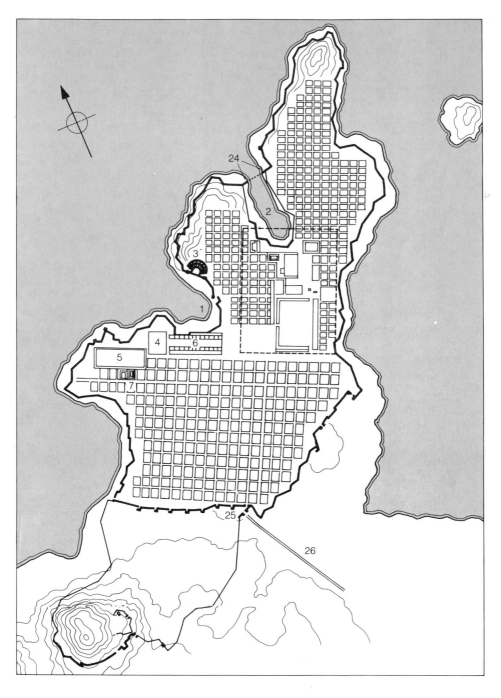

Salamis. But within five years the Milesians had rebuilt their city, and this time they laid it out on a rectangular grid-plan on a long and narrowing south-to-north peninsula with two identations of the sea on its western side. The southernmost of these is now known as the **theatre port** (1) and the second as the **lion port** (2), the latter being the prinicipal harbour of the ancient city.

The impressive and well-preserved **theatre** (3) faces the theatre port on the western side of the peninsula. It was originally erected in the fourth century BC, when it could seat 5,300; but was enlarged during both the Hellenistic and Roman periods, and finally reached its present seating capacity of 15,000 in the Imperial era.

Directly across from the theatre on the south side of the harbour is the **gymnasium** (4), with the **west agora** (5) abutting it on its southwest corner. The **stadium** (6) was erected *c*. 150 BC and rebuilt in the Roman era. The west agora, the last to be built of the city's three market squares, dates from the same period. Just to the south of this agora are the remains of one of the oldest extant monuments in Miletus, the Ionic **Temple of Athena** (7), which dates from the first half of the fifth century BC.

The civic centre of Hellenistic and Roman Miletus was towards the eastern side of the peninsula, extending from a point east of the theatre port up to the southern and inner end of the lion port. The southernmost and largest of the monuments in this complex is the **south agora** (8), an enormous colonnaded courtyard measuring 164 × 196 m

(*Opposite*) General plan of Miletus.
1. theatre port;
2. lion port;
3. theatre;
4. gymnasium;
5. west agora;
6. stadium; 7. Temple of Athena; 24. lion statues; 25. sacred gate; 26. sacred way to Temple at Didyma.

View northwards from the south agora at Miletus.

(538 × 643 ft). The Doric stoas that bordered the courtyard were erected in the second century BC; those on the east and south sides contained shops that alternately opened onto the agora or the surrounding market streets. The main entrance to the agora was on its western side.

Passing through this gateway from the courtyard, one sees immediately on the right a long and narrow stoa stretching off to the north just outside the northwestern stoa of the agora. This stoa, which is 13.4 m (43 ft) wide and 163 m (536 ft) long, was erected in the second century BC as a storage area for the adjacent market-place. Just beyond the south end of this stoa one comes to a small **Temple of Serapis** (9), which dates from the third century AD. This is basilical in form, with a nave and side aisles; the aisles are formed by two rows of five columns each and fronted by a four-columned porch.

A short way beyond the temple one comes to the enormous and well-preserved **Baths of Faustina** (10), the wife of Marcus Aurelius. This is the only building in Miletus that does not fit the Hippodamian plan, for its axes make an angle of approximately 45 degrees with those of the rectangular grid on which the rest of the city was laid out. Two blocks north of the eastern end of the baths there is a fairly large Roman **heroum** (11), with a peristyle of Corinthian columns surrounding a shrine dedicated to an unknown hero. There is a second **heroum** (12) five blocks to the north and two to the east, which dates from the Hellenistic period, with a courtyard surrounding the circular tomb of another unknown hero.

The other buildings of the civic centre are all due north of the agora, whose **propylon** (13) was at the east end of its north stoa. This monumental gateway opened onto a square from whose left side began a grand processional road that was the main avenue of Miletus in the Hellenistic and Roman periods, flanked by some of the most important public buildings in the city.

Outside the propylon, on the right, are the remains of a basilica of the fifth century AD, with a Roman propylon some two centuries older than the rest of the building; in the early Byzantine period this was the cathedral of Christian Miletus. Just to the north of the basilica's propylon are the remains of a monumental three-storied **nymphaeum** (14) of the second century AD.

Relief of a gladiator and a bear from the theatre at Miletus, *c.* 2nd century AD.

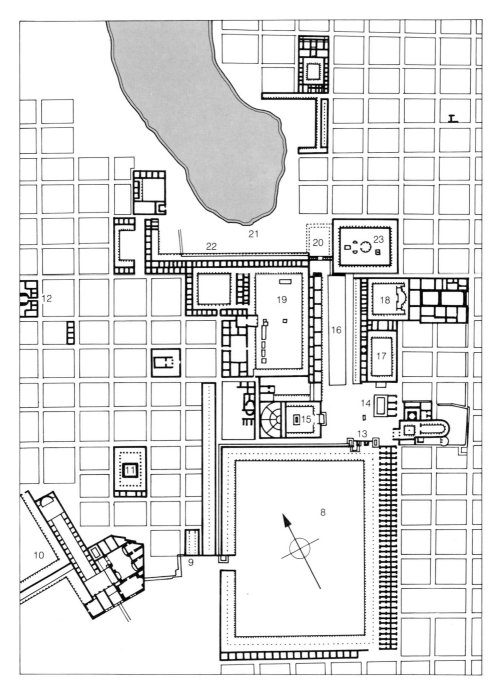

Just to the left of the agora's propylon is the **bouleuterion** (15), which was erected during the period 175–164 BC; from the square one passes through a propylon into a colonnaded courtyard and then into the council chamber itself. Abutting the council chamber on the north are the remains of a small shrine that may have been dedicated to Asclepius, while just to the west of this are the ruins of what is believed to have been the deified emperor's sanctuary, which opened onto the beginning of the **processional way** (16) on its left side. This grand boulevard was 100 m (328 ft) long and 28 m (92 ft) wide, with pavements 5.75 m (19 ft) wide on either side. On the right side of the avenue was an Ionic stoa, with arcaded shops at its rear. Behind this stoa, at the beginning of the avenue, are the remains of a **gymnasium** (17) of the second century BC, with a palaestra on its south side and on the north five rooms where the young athletes engaged in their studies. The splendid four-columned propylon of the gymnasium has recently been restored and re-erected. Just to the north of this is the palaestra of the **Capito Baths** (18), erected by Cn. Vergilius Capito, Procurator of Asia in the reign of the emperor Claudius; the courtyard has two-storeyed Corinthian stoas on all sides except the east, where it opened into the Roman baths themselves.

Across the avenue, on its left side, are the ruins of the **north agora** (19), which was originally built in the classical period and enlarged in both Hellenistic and Roman times. When this agora reached the final stage of its development, in the Imperial Roman era, it was surrounded on all four sides by Corinthian stoas, with two other porticoes opening off its western side, the larger one on the north being a market-place surrounded by shops.

At the northeastern end of the processional way are the remains of a 16-columned portal known as the **harbour gate** (20). This opened into the area around the **lion port** (21), where all of the considerable overseas trade of Miletus was centred. The port quarter was bordered by a portico called the **harbour stoa** (22), erected in the Imperial Roman era. It was a Doric stoa with 75 columns and 36 shops, and extended for nearly 150 m (492 ft) along the south side of the port and for about 20 m (65 ft) along the southwest side.

Adjoining the gateway to the east are the ruins of the oldest and most important sanctuary in Miletus. This is the **Shrine of Apollo Delphinium** (23), the dolphin god, who was the patron deity of Miletus. This cult originated in the belief that Apollo, in the guise of a dolphin, guided the Ionian expeditions when they sailed to establish their overseas colonies. The oldest elements of the shrine are four altars, which date from the sixth century BC; these were part of the archaic Delphinium, destroyed when the Persians levelled Miletus in 494 BC. The stoas that surround these altars date from the early Hellenistic period, with alterations in the Imperial Roman era.

Just beyond the southwest extension of the stoa are the remains of a basilica that served as a synagogue in Roman times (Jewish communities existed in all the Greek cities of western Asia Minor during the Roman period).

The narrow mouth of the lion port is marked by the **statues of two lions** (24) dating from the Hellenistic period. They were excavated from the alluvial earth that the Maeander deposited here across the centuries, marooning this once-great city and leaving it to die in the delta marshes now haunted by its ruins.

The back road from Miletus goes down along the southern-most peninsula of Ionia for some 20 km (12 miles) and brings one to the village of Yenihisar that surrounds ancient Didyma and the ruins of its colossal Temple of Apollo Branchidae. This is perhaps the most impressive classical monument on the Aegean coast of Asia Minor. Its structure is complete except for its colonnade, and three of its columns still stand on their lofty platform, including a pair with their Ionic capitals and architrave still in place.

The name Branchidae derives from the family who served as hereditary priests at the shrine in the archaic period, descendants of a legendary figure called Branchus who was given oracular powers when Apollo fell in love with him.

During the Hellenistic period the oracle of Apollo at Didyma was the most renowned in the Greek world, surpassing even the famed oracle of the god at Delphi. As at Delphi, the priestess of Apollo put herself into a trace-like state called *enthousiasmos* (literally god-withinness), during which it was believed that Apollo entered her body and uttered the prophecies with her voice.

It seems that the Greeks who colonized Miletus took over an ancient Carian shrine at this site about 20 km (12 miles) to

The east front of the Temple of Apollo, Didyma.

the south of their city. The Milesians subsequently linked their city to the shrine with a sacred road flanked by larger-than-life statues of priests, priestesses, lions and sphinxes in the Egyptian style, some of which are now in the British Museum, with one solitary lion remaining on the site.

Excavations have revealed that the earliest Greek construction at Didyma was an altar dating from the eighth century BC, which a century or so later was enclosed in a naiskos and peripteral colonnade. The colossal archaic Temple of Apollo was erected in the decade 560–550 BC, having King Croesus as its principal benefactor. The oracle at Didyma was one of several seers consulted by Croesus before he set out on his ill-fated campaign against Cyrus, but there is no record as to what advice he was given.

The archaic temple at Didyma was destroyed by Xerxes in

479 BC, when he sacked Miletus. But it was rebuilt early in the Hellenistic era by King Seleucus I of Syria. The architects of the second temple were Paeonius of Ephesus and Daphnis of Miletus. The Hellenistic Didymaion, which took five centuries to build and was never fully completed, was designed on an even grander scale than its predecessor. It was the third largest edifice in the ancient Greek world, surpassed in size only by the Artemisium at Ephesus and the Heraeum at Samos.

The stylobate measures 51.13 × 109.41 m (167 × 359 ft); the crepidoma is 3.5 m (11 ft) in height and has 7 steps all the way round except at the middle of the east front, where the *pronaos*, or front porch, is approached by a flight of 14 steps. The temple is of the Ionic order and is of the type known as dipteral decastyle, that is, having a cella surrounded by a double colonnade with ten columns at the ends; the side colonnades each have 21 columns; and the deep eastern pronaos is tetrastyle *in antis*, with two more sets of four columns behind the front row.

Between the front porch and the cella is an antechamber with two Corinthian columns, which served as the *chresmographeion*, or oracle room. This chamber can only be approached by a broad flight of steps leading up from the cella, which is accessible from the pronaos only through a pair of tunnels flanking the stairway. These descending, vaulted structures (among the earliest examples of the Greek use of the vault) give the design an interesting theatricality,

Plan of the Temple of Apollo, Didyma.

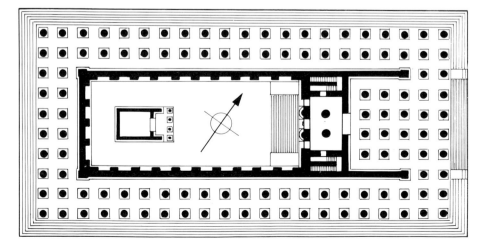

The view east from the cella of the Temple of Apollo, Didyma.

for those approaching the inner sanctuary would first pass through the stygian darkness of one of these tunnels to emerge into the blazing light of the sun-trap cella.

The cella is unroofed like a great open courtyard, with walls more than 22 m (72 ft) high. At the rear of the cella one can see the foundations of a small Ionic prostyle sanctuary which probably housed the sacred bronze cult-statue of Apollo, made by Kanachus of Sicyon. This dates from the first half of the third century BC, the first building phase of the Hellenistic Didymaion. The inner peripteral colonnade of the temple was erected in the second phase, *c*. 200–150 BC; the colonnade in the pronaos dates to the third phase, *c*. 150–100 BC; whereas the outer peripteral colonnade dates to the fourth and final period in the second century AD, which left some of these columns incomplete. The sculptural decoration dates from this period, too.

The Didymaion is particularly beautiful in late afternoon, when the soft oblique light of the falling sun dramatically illuminates the temple, restoring it to something of its former magnificence.

Detail of a column base in the outer colonnade of the Temple of Apollo, Didyma.

THE HERMUS AND MAEANDER VALLEYS

After the Aeolians and Ionians first settled along the Aegean coast, they soon made their way into the interior of the subcontinent along the Hermus and Maeander valleys, founding new cities and Hellenizing older ones. (The Hermus is known in Turkish as the Gediz Çayí, and the Maeander as the Büyük Menderes.) The most important of these classical cities lie in these two valleys, both of which are now traversed by modern highways that have Izmir as their western terminus.

(*Opposite*) The Temple of Aphrodite, Aphrodisias.

The site of Sardis is at Sart, a village 86 km (54 miles) east of Izmir up the Hermus valley. The village is on the east bank of a small stream known to the Greeks as the Pactolus, a tributary of the Hermus which in antiquity carried gold dust down from its source on Mount Tmolus. The **acropolis** (1) of Sardis was on the jagged peak that rises up just over a kilometre southeast of the village centre; the rest of the city was on the lower slopes of this hill to the west and to the north. This was the site of 'golden Sardis', capital of the ancient Kingdom of Lydia.

The Lydian kingdom reached its peak under the dynasty of

SARDIS
(SART)

The Hermus Valley.

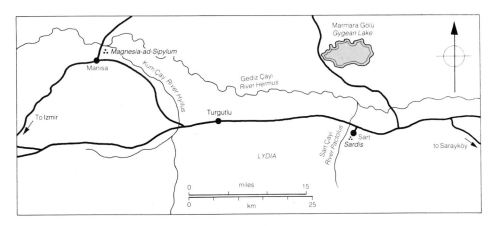

Plan of the ruins of
Sardis.
1. acropolis;
2. Temple of Artemis;
3. Roman civic
centre; 4. House of
Bronzes;
5. synagogue.

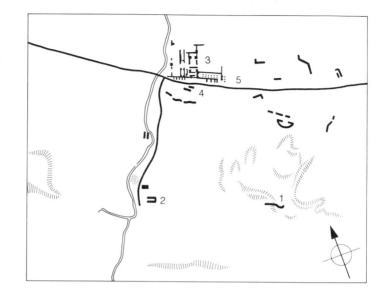

the Mermnadae, which began with the reign of Gyges (*c.* 680–652 BC), who was apparently the first to exploit the gold washed down by the Pactolus, using it to create the earliest-known system of coinage, which made Lydia the richest realm in the world during the archaic period. The kingdom ended in the reign of Croesus (560–546 BC) when he warred with King Cyrus of Persia; Cyrus defeated him and captured Sardis, ending the independent existence of Lydia.

Looking east from the
cella of the Temple of
Artemis, Sardis.

The only substantial monument of ancient Sardis that was visible up until the second decade of the present century was its famous temple, which Herodotus tells us was destroyed when the Ionians set fire to Sardis at the beginning of their revolt against the Persians in 499 BC. Herodotus refers to it as a temple of Cybele, but it has since been discovered that it was dedicated to Artemis (and Zeus), indicating once again that the cult of the ancient Anatolian earth mother was absorbed into that of the Greek fertility goddess.

Ionic capital from the Temple of Artemis, Sardis.

A road leads south from the village centre along the east bank of the Pactolus to the **Temple of Artemis** (2). It is one of the most impressive temples in Asia Minor, particularly when viewed against the background of the ancient acropolis, its fallen fragments now scattered around its cleared stylobate, two columns of its peripteral colonnade still standing, crowned with re-created Ionic capitals.

The original shrine of Artemis on this site was a large sandstone altar just to the west of the temple on its longitudinal axis. This dates from the end of the fifth century BC and is called the 'Lydian Building'. Early in the third century BC, under the Seleucid kings, construction began on the first phase of a west-facing Ionic temple dedicated to Artemis, incorporating the altar at its west end. This was a long and narrow structure with a front porch one-third the length of the inner sanctuary, and with a very shallow rear porch. The cella of this temple was covered with a roof, supported by walls and an internal colonnade in two rows.

Plan of the Temple of Artemis, Sardis.

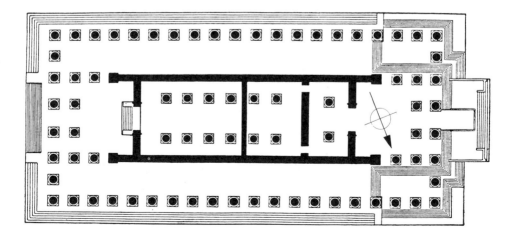

During the second building phase, which lasted from c. 175–150 BC, work was begun on the erection of the outer colonnade, which was to have 8 columns on each of the ends and 20 along the sides, with 6 columns outside its front and rear porches. At that time only 17 columns were erected at the east end of the temple, including the 6 columns in the rear porch. The colonnade and other additions were completed (almost) in the third and final phase of construction, during the reign of Antoninus Pius. The cella was divided into two almost equal halves by an internal cross-wall, with the western half still sacred to Artemis, but with the eastern (rear) section dedicated to the late empress Faustina I, wife of Antoninus Pius, who was deified after her death in AD 141. The row of columns at the west front of the temple was never erected except for one at the southwest corner.

The major excavation area at Sardis in recent years has been just to the east of the village centre in Sart, particularly on the north side of the highway. An enormous **Roman civic centre** (3) has been unearthed there; this was erected after a catastrophic earthquake in AD 17, and it was in continuous use from then on into the early centuries of the Byzantine period. The eastern half of the complex was designed as a gymnasium, whereas the western half comprised its associated baths and athletic facilities. The central area of this complex, the Marble Court, is now being superbly reconstructed, with its monumental two-storeyed arcade adorning the eastern propylon of the courtyard, where one passes from the palaestra into the baths. This court is an outstanding example of the Roman baroque style of architecture, which was beginning to appear about this time. Most of the eastern half of the gymnasium is taken up by the palaestra; this huge colonnaded court, which is also being restored, has a long suite of rooms at its southern end, that were apparently used as dressing-chambers or lecture-halls.

The southern side of the gymnasium was converted in the early Byzantine period into a row of vaulted shops. These faced a similar arcade on the other side of the avenue, which comprised the westernmost stretch of the Royal Persian Road between Susa and Sardis. The quarter of the archaeological site south of the highway here is known as the Lydian Market Area, since this appears to have been the agora of ancient Sardis. The major structure unearthed in this area is called the **House of Bronzes** (4), from the large

Colonnade of the gymnasium, Sardis.

number of bronzes found here, ranging in date from classical times until the early Byzantine era. (These and other antiquities discovered in recent excavations at Sardis are now in the local archaeological museum at Manisa, 43 km (27 miles) by road northeast of Izmir.)

One of the most interesting discoveries made here is the ancient **synagogue** (5). In late Roman times it occupied the long apsidal area in the gymnasium south of the palaestra and adjoining the highway. It is the largest ancient synagogue known, and its size and grandeur are a testimony to the prosperity and eminence of the Jews in Sardis during

Roman times. It seems to date from the years AD 220–50, with renovations as late as the fourth or fifth century AD. Evidence of a much older synagogue comes from the Jewish historian Josephus, writing in the first century AD, who quotes decrees of Julius Caesar and Augustus guaranteeing the religious freedom of the Jewish community in Sardis, who had apparently possessed this right since the early Hellenistic period.

HIERAPOLIS
(PAMUKKALE)

The route that takes one across from the Hermus to the Maeander valley, a drive of 138 km (86 miles) from Sardis, brings one to the Izmir-Denizli highway at Köprübaşí. At this point travellers with time to spare might want to make a detour eastward to Pamukkale, a drive of 43 km (27 miles) from Köprübaşí. Pamukkale is one of the natural wonders of Turkey, standing atop a spectacular cliff turned snow-white from the limestone-laden waters that flow down its sides from the plateau above to the Lycus valley below.

Pamukkale is the site of ancient Hierapolis, the Sacred City, so named because of the many sanctuaries that stood there in ancient times. The only shrines that remain today are a Temple of Apollo and its associated cave-sanctuary of Pluto, god of the underworld. These date from the Hellenistic period, probably from the original foundation by Eumenes II. Most of the other extant monuments on the site date from the Imperial Roman era, most notably the impressive and well-preserved theatre and baths. Hierapolis was a famous spa in Roman times, just as Pamukkale is today; the modern town has an hotel built around the ancient Sacred Pool, at whose bottom one can see classical columns and capitals and other fragments of antiquity.

The Maeander Valley.

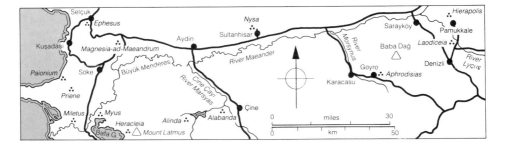

Those making the detour to Pamukkale might also make a slight diversion to visit the site of ancient Laodiceia, of which little remains but scattered ruins. The city was founded in the second quarter of the third century BC by the Seleucid emperor Antiochus II, who named it for his wife Laodicea, whom he divorced in 253 BC. The city is more accurately known as Laodiceia-ad-Lycum, to distinguish it from the many other Laodiceias founded by the Seleucid dynasty.

Heading west from Köprübaşí along the valley of the Maeander the road takes one to the turn-off to Aphrodisias, a drive of 40 km (25 miles); from there the drive southeast to the site is another 35 km (22 miles).

Twenty years ago the picturesque ruins of Aphrodisias were scattered in and around the very pretty village of Geyre, whose houses were built largely from remnants of the ancient city. But the present excavations, which began in 1961 under the direction of Professor Kenan Erim of New York University, have now reached such a scale that the village and its inhabitants have been moved to another site nearby. Some of the superb sculptures unearthed are now exhibited in a new museum, which is located in what was once Geyre's village square, while others can be seen around the archaeological zone, one of the most interesting and beautiful classical sites in all of Turkey.

The excavations at Aphrodisias have unearthed remains of a settlement dating back to *c*. 5,800 BC. The site seems to have been a very ancient shrine of Ishtar, the fertility goddess of Nineveh and Babylon, who was one of the predecessors of Aphrodite, the Greek goddess of love. The earliest Greek sanctuary of Aphrodite on this site dates from the sixth century BC.

The city of Aphrodisias became famous in the late archaic period, and during the next four centuries the cult of Aphrodite spread throughout the Graeco-Roman world from this shrine. She was the mother of Aeneas, the legendary founder of Rome, and her sanctuary here acquired the status of a national shrine among the Romans within half a century after it became part of the Province of Asia.

Aphrodisias also became a famous artistic centre, and its

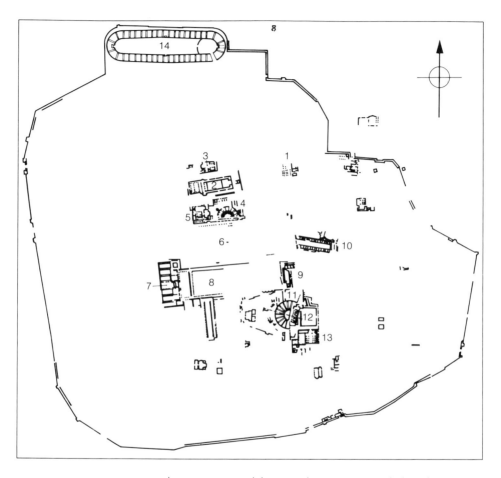

sculptors exported their works to Rome and elsewhere in the classical world. The success of Aphrodisian sculpture was made possible by the proximity of a rich source of marble on the slopes of the nearby mountain, Baba Dağ. The quality of the local statues suggests that master sculptors moved to Aphrodisias from Pergamum after the Attalid dynasty ended in 133 BC. The Aphrodisian school of sculpture reached its peak in the second century AD, continuing at an exceptionally high level right to the end of antiquity.

One of the structures unearthed is the **Tetrapylon** (1), an elaborately sculptured monumental gateway that originally had four rows of four columns each. Part of the pediment is still in place between a pair of spirally fluted monoliths. This handsome gateway was erected in the mid-second century AD, and was probably part of a processional way to the Temple of Aphrodite.

The propylon of Aphrodite's temenos is some 150 m (160 yd) west of the Tetrapylon, with the east front of the temple 15 m (50 ft) beyond it. The present **Temple of Aphrodite** (2) was begun in the first quarter of the first century BC and completed, except for its precinct wall, during the reign of Augustus. The precinct wall was completed during the reign of Hadrian. It is a pseudo-dipteral temple with eight columns at its end and fifteen along its sides. Fourteen of the columns are still standing (see the illustration on p. 78), all but one of them complete with their Ionic capitals, and two groups continue to support fragments of the architrave. The temple was converted into a church in the late fifth century AD, when the edifice was made into a basilica. The foundations of the Hellenistic Temple of Aphrodite have been unearthed within the nave.

On the north side of the temenos of Aphrodite a small complex has recently been excavated. It is thought that this may have been the **gymnasium** (3) of the philosophical school that existed here in the Hellenistic and Roman periods.

There is a large complex of structures on the south side of the temenos, all of them first discovered in 1962. The first of the monuments in this complex to be unearthed was the **odeum** (4), an elegant little theatre with nine rows of seats divided into nine sectors, the ends of the tiers adorned with lion heads. This dates to the second century AD and is one of the best-preserved structures of its type in Asia Minor. The odeum seated 1,700 and would have been used for cultural events as well as meetings of the senate and town council. The floor of the auditorium was covered with a mosaic pavement and the stage-building was adorned with sculptured reliefs and statuary. A backstage corridor opened onto a porticoed square lined with portrait statues of prominent Aphrodisians, many of which are now on exhibit in the local museum. Adjoining the odeum to the northwest is a circular heroum dedicated to an unknown hero, whose ornate sarcophagus is now in the museum.

Just beside the odeum to the west is a **palatial structure** (5) centring on a courtyard with a lovely peristyle of blue-white marble monoliths crowned with Pergamene capitals. It

(*Opposite*) City plan of Aphrodisias.
1. Tetrapylon;
2. Temple of Aphrodite;
3. gymnasium;
4. odeum; 5. palatial structure; 6. agora;
7. Baths of Hadrian;
8. Portico of Tiberius;
9. agora gate complex;
10. Sebasteion;
11. theatre;
12. Tetrasoon;
13. theatre baths;
14. stadium.

has been dated to the third century AD; in the early Byzantine period it became the residence of the Bishop of Caria.

South of the odeum and the bishop's palace are the remains of the splendid Roman **agora** (6), dating from the first century AD. This vast market-place, which measured about 120 × 205 m (393 × 672 ft), was bordered on at least three of its four sides by Ionic stoas, of which a splendid procession of seven columns still stands complete with its capitals and architrave. The western end of this complex has been identified as the **Baths of Hadrian** (7), dating from the years of his reign. These comprise two pairs of large galleries on either side of a huge central hall, the *calidarium*, or steam-room. The chamber to the south of this was the *tepidarium*, a room of intermediate temperature which served as the anteroom to the baths; the chamber to the east was the *apodyterium*, a reception hall and dressing-room, where a number of beautiful sculpures were found in 1965.

Adjoining the Baths of Hadrian to the east is the **Portico of Tiberius** (8), whose splendid Ionic colonnade has now been partially restored. At the southwest corner of this portico is a basilica consisting of a large nave and two side aisles, the whole structure extending south for about 100 m (330 ft). Both the basilica and the portico date from the first century AD, the latter almost certainly from the reign of Tiberius.

At the eastern end of the Portico of Tiberius is a monumental structure known as the **agora gate complex** (9). This edifice, which dates from the late second century AD, appears to have been an elaborate gateway with a massive two-storeyed columnar façade, flanked by projecting towers that were surmounted by colonnaded upper storeys. Inscriptions indicate that the complex was converted into a fountain-house in the fifth century AD.

Another complex has recently been excavated a short way to the northeast of the agora gate. This has been identified as the **Sebasteion** (10), a shrine dedicated to the deified emperor Augustus and his successors in the Julio-Claudian line.

Excavations in the southwestern corner of the site have unearthed the **theatre** (11), which dates from the second half of the first century AD, rebuilt towards the end of the second century AD. It had seats for some 10,000 spectators, with 27 rows of seats still surviving in excellent condition. The most exciting find made in the excavation was that of an

The theatre at Aphrodisias.

archive of inscriptions on the wall of the skene facing the north parodos. The Archive Wall, as it is now called, contains historical inscriptions made in the first half of the third century AD, and records decrees, letters and events going back to the middle of the first century BC.

A large area immediately to the east of the theatre is called the **Tetrasoon** (12), or four-porticoed piazza, centring on a circular altar. It is believed that the Tetrasoon was used as a market-place and shopping-mall, and that it was built in the fourth century AD after the older agora to the northwest had been permanently flooded by the rise in the local water-table. Adjoining the Tetrasoon to the south is an enormous structure known as the **theatre baths** (13), originally built in the late second or early third century AD.

At the northwest corner of the archaeological site one finds the **stadium** (14), the largest and best-preserved structure of its type that has survived from the classical world. The stadium is 262 m (860 ft) long and 59 m (193 ft) across at its widest point. There are about 30 tiers of benches, which seated some 30,000 people. The stadium was built in the first or second century AD and was used principally for athletic events and games, though it was also used for periodic

Colonnaded avenue
in the theatre baths,
Aphrodisias.

The stadium,
Aphrodisias.

competitions in sculpture, evidence of the high esteem in which that art was held in Aphrodisias.

NYSA
(SULTANHISAR)

The drive back west along the Maeander valley passes an interesting archaeological site at Sultanhisar, just 2 km (1 ¼ miles) to the north of the highway. This is the site of ancient Nysa, a little city founded in the first half of the third century BC by the Seleucid emperor Antiochus I. Its surviving edifices date mostly from the Roman period, the most remarkable being the amphitheatre, which is built over the course of a mountain torrent, and the well-preserved library.

At Aydín the route passes the main highway that leads south via Yatağan and Muğla to Marmaris and other ports on Turkey's Mediterranean coast. If one travels west as far as the turn-off to Söke, the highway takes one on a long loop through southern Ionia and around western Caria.

The last stop on the present itinerary is Magnesia-ad-Maeandrum, whose ruins lie beside the road a short distance beyond the turn-off on the final leg to Söke. All that remains of the city today are a short stretch of its Byzantine walls, cut through by the modern highway, and the foundations and architectural fragments of the famous Temple of Artemis Leucophryne, an attribute of the goddess meaning 'White-Browed'.

This is one of two cities in Asia Minor called Magnesia; the other, which has now vanished, was Magnesia-ad-Sipylum, in the valley of the Hermus. The two Magnesias gave the Greeks access to the two great rivers that flowed into the sea from the heart of Anatolia, thus opening up the subcontinent to their trade and commerce.

The oldest sanctuary of Artemis at Magnesia-ad-Maeandrum dates from the sixth century BC. The present sanctuary is an Ionic temple dating to the second century BC, one of the two surviving works of the great Hermogenes. Vitruvius considered Hermogenes' Temple of Artemis Leucophryne to be the archetype of the pseudo-dipteros, a temple surrounded by a wide covered colonnade but without an inner row of columns.

MAGNESIA-AD-MAEANDRUM

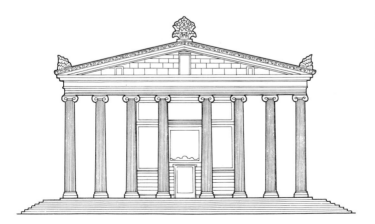

Restoration of the Temple of Artemis Leucophryne, Magnesia-ad-Maeandrum.

The edifice built by Hermogenes is west-facing, for that was the traditional orientation of temples of the ancient fertility goddess in Anatolia. The cult-statue of the goddess stood near the back of the cella, looking out towards her altar in front of the temple. This altar was a scaled-down version of the great Altar of Zeus at Pergamum. When the remains of the altar were uncovered, in 1891–3, fragments of the 200 m (653 ft) long frieze from the temple were also found, some reliefs of which are now exhibited in the Louvre and the Istanbul Archaeological Museum.

The Temple of Artemis Leucophryne was much admired in Rome as well as elsewhere in the classical world; Strabo, a contemporary of Vitruvius, was of the opinion that it was superior to the Artemisium at Ephesus 'in the fine proportion of the skill exhibited in the structure of the enclosure'.

The excavations of 1891–3 also uncovered an enormous agora just to the west of the Temple of Artemis, but this has since been covered up again by the silt of the Maeander, as have several other structures discovered at that time. The most important of these was a small Ionic temple within the southern half of the agora; this was dedicated to Zeus Sosipolis and to Tyche, the goddess of fortune, and it too was designed by Hermogenes.

THE BELEVI
MONUMENT

Travellers returning to Izmir from the Maeander valley can make a short and very interesting detour 11 km (7 miles) beyond Selçuk, where a turn-off to the right brings one after a kilometre or so to the Belevi Monument. This is an immense funerary monument, part of which is carved out of a huge cube of rock on the hillside and the rest constructed with both Doric and Corinthian elements. The main chamber of the sepulchre contained a sarcophagus, now in the Izmir Museum, its lid surmounted by a sculpture representing the deceased. The figure has been identified as the Seleucid emperor Antiochus II, who died at Ephesus in 246 BC.

CARIA

The Maeander River marked the ancient boundary between Ionia and Caria, the wild and beautiful region that forms the southwestern extremity of Asia Minor.

The highway that leads south from Izmir via Selçuk and Söke takes one into the heart of Caria at Milas (82 km/51 miles from Söke), site of the old Carian capital of Mylasa. *En route* the highway passes the sites of two ancient Carian cities, Heracleia-under-Latmus and Euromus, whose ruins are among the most evocative in all of Asia Minor.

Heracleia, 46 km (28 miles) from Söke, is at the eastern tip of Bafa Gölü, the shallow lake that was once the inner end of the Latmian Gulf. The ruins lie under Mount Latmus, hence its

HERACLEIA-UNDER-LATMUS

The Carian shore.

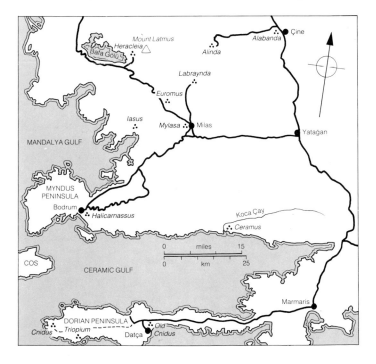

93

name. Heracleia-under-Latmus was one of the first cities to be laid out on a rectangular grid-plan, recognizable even today among the tumbled ruins of the ancient city. Most of the structures one sees here today are Hellenistic, the most prominent being the defence walls, the Temple of Athena and the agora. The theatre and the public baths date from Imperial Roman times. The most fascinating monument at Heracleia is the rock-hewn cave-sanctuary known as the Tomb of Endymion. Its date is uncertain, but it may have been erected early in the Byzantine era, when Christian anchorites apparently rediscovered a more ancient sepulchre on the Latmian Gulf under Mount Latmus.

EUROMUS

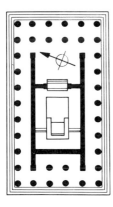

Euromus is 19 km (12 miles) south of Lake Bafa along the highway. The only monument of any consequence that has survived from this once-important town is its Temple of Zeus, which stands embowered in an olive grove a few hundred metres to the left of the road. This is a Corinthian edifice dating from no later than the first half of the second century AD, perhaps from the reign of Hadrian. Its peripteral colonnade had six columns at the ends and eleven on the flanks, with four more columns in its front porch and two between the *antae* of the very shallow rear porch; the cult-statue of Zeus was contained within a naiskos in the cella. Sixteen of the temple's columns are still standing with their splendid Corinthian capitals and architrave. Twelve of the surviving columns have tablets with dedicatory inscriptions.

Plan of the Temple of Zeus, Euromus.

The Temple of Zeus, Euromus.

Twelve kilometres (7 miles) farther on the highway comes to a crossroads at Milas, the ancient Mylasa, with the left fork leading to Yatağan, the right to Bodrum, and the secondary road straight ahead going to the village of Ören on the Ceramic gulf, the site of ancient Ceramus.

The original site of Mylasa is believed to have been at Peçin Kale, a great flat-topped rock that rises to a height of nearly 220 m (722 ft) some 5 km (3 miles) south of Milas. Excavations have revealed that this unassailable eyrie was first settled as early as 2,000 BC, and it remained inhabited until the fourth century BC, when the new site of Mylasa was laid out on the plain to its north.

There is little left of ancient Mylasa to be seen in the modern town of Milas. Strabo writes that the Mylasians had three temples dedicated to Zeus, two of them in Mylasa itself and the third in Labraynda, on a mountain top site 13 km (8 miles) north of the city. A solitary remnant of one of these temples stands in a public garden in the centre of Milas near the town hall; this is a fluted column complete with its Corinthian capital, standing on a stepped podium that is undoubtedly part of the crepidoma of the temple. There is a panel on the column where the dedicatory inscription would have been recorded, but this has long since been effaced.

Another remnant of ancient Mylasa is the splendid portal called Baltalí Kapí, the Gate of the Axe, an almost perfectly preserved Roman gateway, probably erected just before the beginning of the Christian era. It takes its name from the ritual double-axe, or *labyrs*, represented on the keystone of the round arch on its outer side. This gate led to the Sacred Way that extended from Mylasa to Labraynda, the great Carian shrine on the mountain-top north of the city.

There is a rough road from Milas up to the mountainside to its north to the site of Labraynda, following the course of the ancient Sacred Way from Mylasa, whose original paving-stones can be seen along the way. The majestic ruins of Labraynda stand serenely alone on the terraces of its exceedingly steep site. The shrine was dedicated to Zeus Stratius, whose festival was celebrated here by all of the Carian people in their national sanctuary. This was where the Carians made their last stand against the Persians at the

The Temple of Zeus at Labraynda, with Andron A in the background to the left.

The Roman tomb known as Gümüşkesen.

end of the Ionian Revolt in 494 BC. The principal monument on the site is the Temple of Zeus, which was begun by Mausolus and completed by his brother Idrieus, who ruled Caria in the years 351–344 BC. This is an Ionic temple with six columns at its ends and eight along its sides, and with a pair of columns *in antis* in its very shallow rear porch. Other interesting and well-preserved structures on the site are the royal dining-halls, known as Androns A and B, which were also erected by Mausolus and Idrieus.

GÜMÜŞKESEN

The most remarkable monument in the immediate vicinity of Milas is the Roman tomb known locally as Gümüşkesen, which is on the outskirts of the town on the road leading to the west. This is a splendid funerary monument dating from just before the beginning of the Christian era. It is a two-storeyed structure, with a massive burial chamber forming the lower level. The tomb itself is entered by a door on the western side, and above this there is a Corinthian porch, with square piers on the corners and between them pairs of columns, the whole surmounted by a pyramidal roof of ingenious construction. It is thought that the design was based on that of the Mausoleum in Halicarnassus.

OTHER NORTHERN CARIAN SITES

Milas is a good base for visiting other sites in the north of Caria, most notably Iasus, Alinda and Alabanda. Iasus is on the coast just to the west of Milas, and the other two sites are in the Carian hills to the west and north of Labraynda. Alabanda and Alinda can be reached by jeep from Çine, which is midway along the road between Yatağan and Aydín. Yatağan is 42 km (26 miles) from Milas, and Çine is 38 km (23 miles) from Yatağan. All of these sites have interesting monuments, and the settings of Alinda and Alabanda are extremely beautiful.

HALICARNASSUS (BODRUM)

The right fork of the highway at Milas leads down the Myndus peninsula to Bodrum, the ancient Halicarnassus, a drive of 72 km (45 miles). The principal monument of Bodrum is its magnificent Crusader castle of St. Peter, built by the Knights of St. John; it was begun in 1402 and completed toward the end of that century. The castle now houses the

Museum of Underwater Archaeology, which has on exhibition objects found both at underwater and mainland sites. One exhibit of particular interest is a sculptured slab from one of the friezes of the Mausoleum, the most famous monument of ancient Halicarnassus.

Halicarnassus was one of the six cities founded by the Dorians on the southwestern corner of Anatolia and its offshore islands in their migration early in the first millennium BC. The Dorian colonies formed a league originally known as the Hexapolis, or Six Cities, but this became the Pentapolis, or Five Cities, after Halicarnassus was expelled because of an offence committed by one of its citizens, an incident related by Herodotus in Book I of his *Histories*.

The greatest period in the history of Halicarnassus came

Reconstruction of the Mausoleum at Halicarnassus.

during the reign of Mausolus (377–353 BC). Mausolus had transferred his capital from Mylasa to Halicarnassus, ruling from there over a realm that included all of Caria and considerable portions of Ionia, Lydia and Lycia, as well as the islands of Rhodes, Cos and Chios. At that time Mausolus quadrupled the population of his capital by transporting to Halicarnassus all of the people from the six ancient Lelegian towns on the Myndus peninsula. Mausolus then enclosed his new capital with a great circuit of powerful defence walls studded with massive watchtowers at regular intervals, along with three separate walled citadels. He also adorned Halicarnassus with splendid edifices to suit its new role as capital of the Carian kingdom; the most famous of these monuments was the Mausoleum, which he designed as a great Carian shrine dedicated to himself and his sister-wife, Artemisia II. Mausolus began work on this sepulchre before his death in 353 BC, and Artemisia completed it before her own death two years later.

Statue of a member of Mausolus' family, which stood between the columns of the Mausoleum at Halicarnassus.

Travellers to Bodrum had long reported that many fragments of the ancient Mausoleum were to be seen built into the walls of the castle of St. Peter, but the site of the great sepulchre remained unknown until its foundations and some of its sculptures were unearthed in the years 1856–9. Recent excavations have determined the dimensions of the Mausoleum's *peribolos*, or precinct wall, which formed a rectangle measuring 242 m (794 ft) from north to south and 105.5 m (346 ft) from east to west. Enough is now known to allow for a fairly certain reconstruction of the monument.

According to Pliny, the lower part of the structure consisted of a high podium (which served as the basement of the monument), estimated by Dinsmoor to measure 32.0 × 38.7 m (108 × 127 ft). Above this stood a peristyle of 36 Ionic columns, which it is thought were arranged with eleven on the sides and nine on the ends. Above the portico was a pyramidal roof of 24 steps, surmounted by a *quadriga*, or four-horse chariot. The Mausoleum was also adorned with three sculptured friezes, the positions of which are still in question; these represented a Centauromachy, an Amazonomachy, and an unidentified scene with charioteers.

The architects of the Mausoleum were Pythius and Satyrus and the sculptors were Bryaxis, Leochares, Timotheus and Scopas, each of whom is believed to have worked on one face of the monument. Scopas is thought to have worked on

Colossal marble horse from the four-horse chariot, which stood on the apex of the Mausoleum at Halicarnassus.

Relief showing Greeks fighting Amazons from the Mausoleum at Halicarnassus.

the east face, which was at the front of the Mausoleum, and it is possible that Pythius himself may have carved the quadriga. The British Museum has sculptures from all three of these friezes, as well as other works, including the colossal statues thought to be Mausolus' relatives, which stood between the columns. The panel of the frieze now exhibited in the Bodrum museum shows a scene from an Amazonomachy, in which a naked Greek warrior is about to slay a fallen Amazon maiden. The most notable of all the sculptures from the Mausoleum is the statue of a man (once thought to be Mausolus himself), particularly the magnificent head with its intense and brooding expression.

The theatre of ancient Halicarnassus has recently been excavated and is now being restored. This also appears to date from the reign of Mausolus, whose ancient capital is thus beginning to re-emerge from its ruins.

CNIDUS

Travellers proceeding on from Bodrum to Marmaris have a choice of two routes, either along the highway or by chartered boat, the latter route now being popularized by Turkish tourism as the Mavi Yol, or Blue Voyage. The most important site along this route is Cnidus; this is best approached by sea, for it is on the tip of the very long Dorian peninsula, directly south of Bodrum across the width of the Gökova Körfezi, known to the Greeks as the Ceramic Gulf.

The original site of Cnidus, founded early in the first millennium BC in the Dorian migration, was halfway along the southern coast of the peninsula, near what is now the coastal village of Datça. The Cnidians abandoned that city c. 360 BC and moved to the present site at the western end of the peninsula, undoubtedly because the promontory there was better suited for defence and Aegean maritime trade. The western end of the Dorian peninsula was known in antiquity as the Triopium promontory, named after the Argive hero who was the legendary founder of the city. This promontory was the site of the sanctuary of Triopian Apollo, where a great annual festival, including athletic games, was celebrated by the cities of the Dorian League.

Although the shrine of Triopian Apollo was on Cnidian territory, the principal deity of Cnidus was not Apollo but Aphrodite. According to Pausanius, she was worshipped here in her temple as Aphrodite Euploia, the goddess of good sailing, an appropriate dedication for a city of mariners such as Cnidus. The Temple of Aphrodite was probably built soon after the Cnidians moved their city to the new site on the Triopium promontory in the mid-fourth century BC, in which case the cult-statue of the goddess would have been the famous nude figure of Aphrodite by the renowned Athenian sculptor Praxiteles. This statue is the earliest-known freestanding figure of a naked woman in the Greek world.

A team of American archaeologists under Professor Iris Love began excavating Cnidus in the mid-1960s. Among the important monuments identified in this excavation was the circular base of a temple, along with a marble fragment inscribed with the first four letters of the name Praxiteles and the first three of Aphrodite. Consequently the structure was identified with certainty as the Temple of Aphrodite in which the Praxitelian statue of Cnidian Aphrodite stood. Less certain by far is Professor Love's claim to have discovered the head of this statue in the basement of the British Museum, where it had been stored among the many marbles shipped back to England from the excavations at Cnidus in 1856-7. The authorities at the museum insist that the rather battered head is that of Persephone; this was discovered in the Sanctuary of Demeter at Cnidus, and was attributed to the Praxitelean school rather than to the great sculptor himself.

The statue of Demeter from the Sanctuary of Demeter at Cnidus.

Aside from the Sanctuaries of Aphrodite and Demeter, excavations at Cnidus have also unearthed the remains of a small Corinthian temple dating from the reign of Hadrian. Other monuments include a bouleuterion, an agora, a Doric Stoa, a Temple of the Muse and a lighthouse which must have been one of the principal landmarks in the Aegean, marking the southwesternmost point in Asia Minor.

LYCIA

Lycia is the most beautiful and fascinating region along the Turkish coast, and also the most mysterious and enchanting. The tomb-haunted Lycian landscape has bewitched travellers ever since Charles Fellows first explored its ancient sites in the years 1838–44, discovering the magnificent sculptured sepulchres that are now in the British Museum. Fellows records the excitement of his discoveries in a journal entry dated 28 April 1840:

> 'What a wonderful people the ancient Greeks were! This mountain country was literally strewed with cities and stately towers, which stand uninjured and unoccupied two thousand years after their builders were removed!'

Much more is known about the Lycians now than when Fellows explored their ruined cities. It is now certain that they were an Anatolian people called the Lukka, mentioned in both Egyptian and Hittite records dating to the middle of the second millennium BC.

Archaeologists have uncovered evidence of human habitation dating back to the Bronze Age at a number of Lycian sites, most notably in the dig near Elmalí. The site is on the slopes of Bey Dağ, the highest mountain in Lycia, known to

(*Opposite*) The Tomb of Amyntas, Telmessus.

The Lycian shore.

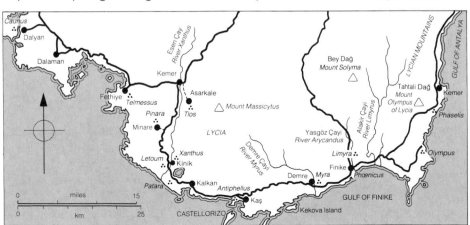

103

the Greeks as Mount Solyma. This is the ancient homeland of Homer's Solymoi, the ancestors of the Lycians.

The people of southwestern Anatolia retained their identity even after they were dominated by the Greeks and Romans, and they continued to be known as Lycians up until late antiquity. In Strabo's time the Lycians were still a distinct, if thoroughly Hellenized, people. Under Roman rule they still had considerable national autonomy and settled their affairs as members of the Lycian League. This was founded in 167 BC, though it probably perpetuated an ancient ethnic union of the Lycian people.

Lycia is much more accessible today than it was two decades ago, before the completion of the new coastal highway and the opening of the international airport at Dalaman; these, together with the cruises of the Mavi Yol, have now opened the Lycian shore to international tourism, though it still retains much of its haunting mystery.

The international airport is named after the Dalaman Nehri, the River Indus of antiquity, which forms the ancient boundary between Caria and Lycia. The Lycian coast extends all the way from there to Antalya, where Lycia ends and Pamphylia begins. The principal sites are all on or near the coast in western Lycia, their maritime approaches being the ports at Marmaris, Fethiye, Kalkan, Kaş and Finike; the sites on the inhospitable eastern Lycian shore are best approached via the coastal highway.

CAUNUS

From Dalaman one can make a short excursion westward along the main highway to the signposted turn-off that brings one to Dalyan, which is about 20 km (12 miles) from the airport, and thence to the site of ancient Caunus. Dalyan is a tiny port on the left bank of the reed-fringed river that winds its way to the sea from Lake Köceğiz, which is fed by one of the many branches of Dalaman Nehri. Caunus is on the right bank of the river, so that it is technically a Carian town, although the rock-hewn tombs in its necropolis are typically Lycian. To reach the site of the ancient city, one must hire a boat at Dalyan. At the beginning of the forty-five minute journey one can see an impressive group of temple-tombs carved into cliff-face opposite the port; this is the necropolis of Caunus, whose acropolis surmounts the Gibraltar-like rock around which the river makes a great bend on its way back to the site of the ancient city. The boat lands one on the shore to the northwest of the acropolis, and from there it is a short walk to the ancient city. The city is laid out on the slope of a hill leading down to its ancient port, which is now just a stagnant pond surrounded by the marsh that cuts off Caunus from the sea. One path leads from the landing-place to the uppermost part of the city, the principal monuments there being the Roman theatre and baths and an early Byzantine basilica. Another path leads down from the baths to a complex of structures that includes a *templum-*

The *templum-in-antis* at Caunus.

in-antis and a semicircular sanctuary with three columns of its outer colonnade still standing, along with part of the entablature. Beyond this at the centre of the port there is another complex consisting of a porticoed square and an exceptionally well-preserved fountain-house dedicated to Vespasian. Past this at the far left corner of the port there is a quite unique monument called the Tholos, probably a nymphaeum, which consists of a circular basin of white marble standing beside a large rectangular pool.

TELMESSUS (FETHIYE)

The largest town on the Lycian coast today is Fethiye, 58 km (36 miles) from Dalaman, which is set on a beautiful bay at the eastern end of its magnificent gulf. Fethiye occupies the site of ancient Telmessus, whose necropolis can still be seen just outside the town to the north, where the cliffs are pockmarked with rock-hewn Lycian tombs carved out of the sheer face of the precipice. The grandest of these funerary monuments are designed in the form of temple façades, the most notable being the Tomb of Amyntas, dating from the fourth century BC. Others are in the form of sarcophagi patterned on ancient Lycian cottages, such as the splendid one outside the town hall of Fethiye.

TLOS

Past Fethiye the highway leads east and goes inland as far as the turn-off to Kemer, a drive of 23 km (14 miles), where the main road turns south to head down the Xanthus valley. The turn-off takes one across the river to a crossroads, where the main road leads inland, the one to the left goes into Kemer, and the one to the right heads south along the Xanthus valley to Tlos, one of the great cities of ancient Lycia, which is about 15 km (9 miles) from the turn-off. (This road is not signposted, and so one must ask for directions along the way.) This was the route taken by Charles Fellows in 1839, on the journey in which he discovered Tlos and the other ancient cities along the Xanthus valley, recording his impressions in the journal that became one of the enduring classics in the travel literature of Asia Minor:

'The whole ride down this upper valley is beautiful and varies continually; its scenery, on approaching the bold and Greek-like situation of the ancient city of Tlos, is strikingly picturesque.'

The site of Tlos is indeed picturesque and grand. Its acropolis-hill is dominated by a medieval fortress perched 500 m (1,637 ft) above the Xanthus valley, with the river shining sky-blue 5 km (3 miles) to the west as the eagle flies, while looming further to the west is the majestic peak of Ak Dağ, the Massicytus of antiquity, its summit nearly 3,024 m (10,000 ft) above sea-level.

The final stretch of the approach road brings one to Asarkale, a little hamlet built within and from the ruins of Tlos, dominated by the towering acropolis-hill with its rock-hewn Lycian tombs. The most remarkable of the funerary monuments at Tlos is one known as the Tomb of Bellerophon. This takes its name from the relief in the porch of the sepulchre, where the Corinthian hero Bellerophon is shown riding on his winged horse Pegasus, given to him by his ancestor Poseidon. This sepulchre was probably built for a prince of the royal line at Tlos who claimed descent from Bellerophon, the mythical founder of Lycia.

Other structures of ancient Tlos can be seen in the fields flanking the road that continues above the village, with a long and narrow portico preceding a gymnasium-baths complex and then the agora on the right, and higher up on the left the well-preserved theatre, from which there is a dramatic view of the acropolis and its tombs against the background of the Xanthus valley.

After visiting Tlos one must return to the Kemer crossroads to get back on to the main highway leading south. About halfway down the valley, some 20 km (12 miles) beyond the crossroads, there is a turn-off to the right signposted for Pinara, one of the principal cities of ancient Lycia. The road leads to the village of Minare, just outside of which there is a car-park where the *bekci*, or watchman, has his station. One would be well-advised to hire him as a guide, for the ruins are far above the village and difficult of access.

The site of Pinara, which has never been excavated, is the most spectacular of all the ancient cities in Lycia. The main part of the city is perched on a narrow shelf of rock that extends north-south high above the plain, with its acropolis crowning the flat top of a table-rock 500 m (1,637 ft) high. The entire face of this pinkish red rock is pockmarked with hundreds of tombs, most of them just rectangular hollows

PINARA

A rock-cut tomb in the south necropolis at Pinara.

carved out of the sheer face of the cliff. More elaborate tombs of the temple type are carved in the rock face of the south necropolis just below the city-terrace, and one passes these in the arduous climb up from the car-park outside Minare. The most notable monument in the south necropolis is the Royal Tomb; this is of particular interest because the reliefs that flank its entrance are representations of an ancient walled city which Charles Fellows believed to be Pinara itself, although modern scholars are sceptical.

The vertiginous path finally brings one to the south end of the city-terrace, an extraordinary Shangri-La of mottled grey stone. Among its ruined edifices is a Temple of Aphrodite with a peripteral colonnade of heart-shaped columns, its threshold marked with a relief depicting a very elongated phallus. Other structures in its vicinity include a Temple of Artemis that stands on a lofty podium overlooking the Xanthus valley. From there one has a clear view of the perfectly preserved Roman theatre of Pinara, whose auditorium is carved out of a hillside below the city-terrace to the east, with lordly Massicytus rising above it.

THE LETOUM

Seventeen km (11 miles) south of the turn-off to Pinara there is a turn-off on the right to the Letoum, the principal sanctuary of ancient Lycia, which is 4 km (2½ miles) from the highway. The name of the sanctuary derives from Leto, the mother of Artemis and Apollo, the divine twins fathered by Zeus. This sanctuary eluded Fellows during his exploration of Lycia, and it was first discovered and identified by Hoskyn in 1840. A French archaeological team under Professor Henri Metzger began working on the site in 1950, and has now identified the principal surviving monuments.

The approach road to the archaeological site ends in front of the Roman theatre. The **theatre** (1) is very well preserved, and the gateways to its two *parodoi*, or side entrances, are the most handsome in Asia Minor. The entrance to the archaeological site is just to the right of the theatre, where the local *bekci* has set up a table and bench under a venerable olive tree, a perfect spot from which to survey the Letoum and identify its monuments.

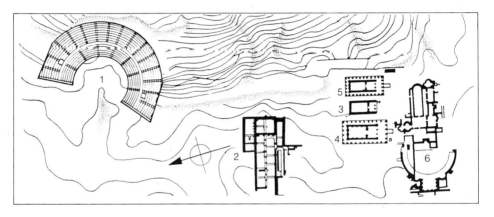

Plan of the Letoum.
1. theatre; 2. agora;
3. Temple of Artemis;
4. Temple of Leto;
5. Temple of Apollo;
6. nymphaeum.

Theatre gateway at the Letoum.

The half-submerged complex of ruins that occupies the northern half of the site is the **agora** (2), the bases of its peripheral colonnade almost completely intact just below the surface of the stagnant pool of moss-green water that has seeped in from the nearby Xanthus River, its column drums and other architectural members neatly stacked on the solid ground around it. Just beyond the agora one comes to a triad of temples that forms the heart of the Letoum. All three temples face south towards another half-submerged complex, the excavated site of an enormous nymphaeum, which appears to have been fed by a sacred spring associated with the myth of Leto and her divine twins.

The smaller and much older temple in the middle has been identified by an inscription as a sanctuary of Artemis, with current opinion being that the one to its west was dedicated to Leto and the eastern one to Apollo. The inscription dates the **Temple of Artemis** (3) to 358 BC; the other temples are believed to have been erected in the third or second century BC. The **Temple of Leto** (4), the largest and best-preserved of the three, is of the Ionic order and has a peristyle of six by eleven columns, with two columns *in antis* in its front porch. The Temple of Artemis is also Ionic, but the **Temple of Apollo** (5) is Doric. At the centre of the latter temple there is a perfectly preserved floor mosaic representing the symbols of Leto's children: the lyre of Apollo, god of music, and the bow and arrow of Artemis, goddess of the hunt.

The **nymphaeum** (6) is an impressive structure dating from the reign of Hadrian, its principal remnant being a semi-circular pool with a diameter of 27 m (88 ft). This stands on the site of a much earlier shrine of the nymphs which, according to tradition, is where Leto stopped to drink after she gave birth to Artemis and Apollo.

XANTHUS

Two kilometres beyond the turn-off to the Letoum the highway crosses the Xanthus River and then enters the village of Kíník. At the first crossroads within the village there is a turn-off to the left for the site of ancient Xanthus, whose ruins are immediately evident in their splendid site overlooking the fertile delta of the most beautiful river in western Asia Minor. The approach road takes one past the Arch of Vespasian, the entrance to the ancient city; a short way

beyond that is a parking-lot at the centre of the archaeological site, just opposite the Roman theatre and the agora.

Xanthus was the capital of Lycia throughout antiquity, first
mentioned by Herodotus in his account of the Persian
invasion of Lycia in 546 BC, when the Xanthians immolated
themselves in their city rather than surrender to Harpagus the
Mede. The Xanthians repeated this act of heroism in 42 BC,
when they burned down their city around their heads rather
than surrender to a Roman army led by Brutus.

This was not the end of Xanthus, for the survivors returned
to rebuild their city on the same site, so that in Imperial
Roman times it once again became the leading state in
Lycia, and indeed survived on into the Byzantine era as a
bishopric under the Metropolitan of Myra. But by the time
that Xanthus was rediscovered by Charles Fellows, in 1838,

City plan of Xanthus.
1. The site of the
Nereid Monument;
2. pillar-tomb;
3. Tomb of the
Harpies; 4. Xanthian
Stele; 5. theatre;
6. Palace of the
Lycian kings;
7. Temple of Artemis;
8. defence wall;
9. pillar-tomb;
10. Payava
Sarcophagus.

the site had been long abandoned. Fellows excavated Xanthus in three campaigns between 1839 and 1844, shipping all the antiquities he found back to England, where they are now on exhibit in the British Museum.

The site then lay undisturbed until 1950, when a team of French archaeologists began their work here. The French excavations have unearthed structures representing the entire span of existence of Xanthus, ranging from the original Lycian fortress-town of the eighth century BC to the Roman city and the medieval Byzantine bishopric of the twelfth century AD. Here, as elsewhere in Lycia, the most interesting remains are the funerary monuments, although all of these in Xanthus have either been carted away or stripped of their original sculptural decoration.

The **Nereid Monument** (1) stood on a high hill to the right of the main gate (see the illustration on p. 13), where the road up from the valley below enters the ancient city. This richly decorated Ionic monument, erected in the late fifth century BC, was discovered by Fellows in 1838. It had been thrown down by an earthquake and fragments were scattered over the hillside. These were brought to the British

Reconstruction of the Nereid Monument, Xanthus.

112

Museum in 1842. As reconstructed in the museum, the tomb is designed in the form of a small tetrastyle temple, with six columns along the sides in addition to the four at the ends, and it stands on a high podium decorated with two friezes.

Between the columns there are superb statues of the Nereids from which the monument takes its name, although they are now thought to be aurae, or personifications of the sea breezes. The elegant Ionic capitals closely resemble those in the Athenian Erechtheion, which has led scholars to speculate that the architect of the Nereid Monument was an Athenian, hired by a Xanthian noble who was familiar with the art and architecture of classical Athens. (The cities of Asia Minor were always in close cultural contact with the rest of the Greek world.) The style of the sculptural decoration is close to that of Attic works of the fifth century BC; but the subject-matter of the reliefs is the life and victories of a Xanthian noble.

A nereid or aura from the Nereid Monument, Xanthus.

The two most important of the funerary monuments that remain in Xanthus stand side-by-side next to the Roman theatre. One of them is a **pillar-tomb** (2), a handsome sarcophagus of the fourth century BC standing on a tall platform. Beside this is the famous **Tomb of the Harpies** (3), a tall monolith supporting a sarcophagus in the form of a chest decorated with sculptures in low relief. (The relief *in situ* is a plaster copy of the original, which is in the British Museum.) The so-called Harpies from which the tomb takes its name are actually Sirens, winged creatures that were half-woman and half-bird, who are shown here conducting the souls of the dead to the Underworld.

Beside the road at the northeast corner of the Roman agora is the famous **Xanthian Stele** (4), a pillar-tomb with an inscription of over 250 lines written in both Greek and Lycian. This has been one of the most important sources for the decipherment of the Lycian language, and it also records information about the history of Lycia in the last third of the fifth century BC.

Relief of a harpy from the Tomb of the Harpies, Xanthus.

The **theatre** (5), which dates from the mid-second century AD, is built in against the northeast face of the Lycian acropolis. The oldest ruins on this acropolis are those of a **palace of the Lycian kings** (6), destroyed at the time of the Persian conquest, *c.* 540 BC. All the Lycian buildings on the acropolis, including a **Temple of Artemis** (7), were replaced

View of the theatre at Xanthus, with a pillar-tomb and the Tomb of the Harpies in the background.

by the Byzantine structures one sees today.

Xanthus was enclosed by a **defence wall** (8) which is still standing along its eastern side, where the fortifications extend northward to join those slanting down from the northern acropolis, which was the citadel of Xanthus during the Hellenistic, Roman and Byzantine periods. The south-eastern slope of this acropolis was apparently the principal necropolis of Lycian Xanthus, as evidenced by the number of sarcophagi and rock-hewn tombs one sees there. The most splendid of these is an almost perfectly preserved **pillar-tomb** (9) of the fourth century BC; this stands just above the ruins of the famous **Payava Sarcophagus** (10), dated to the mid-fourth century BC, whose reliefs are now in the British Museum.

The site of Patara is approached by a turn-off on the east side of the Xanthus delta, where the highway passes south of Ova Gölü just before it reaches the town of Kalkan 77 km (48 miles) from Finike.

The ruins of Patara are scattered around the periphery of the marshes that were once its harbour, long since silted-up by the Xanthus River. On entering the archaeological zone

PATARA

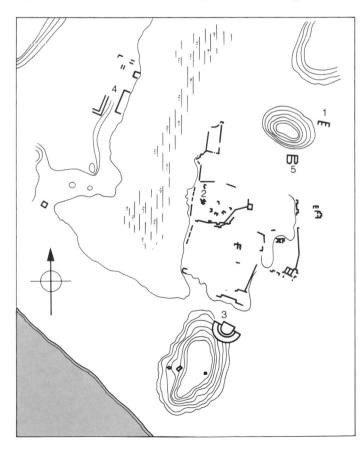

Plan of Patara.
1. propylon;
2. Corinthian temple;
3. theatre;
4. granary;
5. mausoleum.

one is confronted with one of the grandest sights in Asia Minor, a perfectly preserved Roman **propylon** (1) with three great round-arched portals; its dedicatory inscription records that the gateway was built *c*. AD 100 by 'the people of Patara, metropolis of the Lycian nation'.

Patara was renowned in antiquity for its oracle, a priestess of Apollo, who apparently was in residence during the winter months only. This was one of the oldest shrines in Asia Minor, mentioned by Herodotus at the end of his account of the oracles of Egypt and Babylonia. The Temple of Apollo has never been identified, although some authorities have suggested that its site may be the low hillock just to the southeast of the propylon, where some Attic pottery of the classical period has been unearthed. Patara has never been excavated systematically, and the only sanctuary that has survived is a small **Corinthian temple** (2), dating from the second century AD, about 400 m to the southwest of the gateway.

The Roman **theatre** (3) is set into the northern side of a hill that rises above the long sandy beach; and from its upper tier one commands a panoramic view of the entire site. On the western side of the harbour one can see an enormous and well-preserved **granary** (4), one of the most impressive ancient structures on the Turkish coast, a vast two-storeyed vaulted hall 25 m (82 ft) wide and 60 m (196 ft) long. This was built by Hadrian in AD 125, when he visited Patara on his grand tour of Greece and Asia Minor. A short way to the north of the granary are the ruins of a large and extremely well-built Roman **mausoleum** (5), designed in the form of a Corinthian pseudo-dipteral temple. There is another monumental Roman tomb on the opposite side of the river, just to the right of the road as one approaches the site.

ANTIPHELLUS
(KAŞ)

Twenty-seven km (17 miles) beyond Kalkan the coastal highway brings one to Kaş. This is the southernmost town on the Lycian coast of Turkey, and its beautiful harbour is almost enclosed at its outer end by the small and lonely Greek island of Castellorizzo. Kaş has been identified as the site of Antiphellus, an ancient Lycian town whose archaeological record dates back to the sixth century BC. Antiphellus was originally just the port for Phellus, but early in the Hellenistic period it became one of the most important harbours on the southern coast of Asia Minor, eclipsing its mother-city. The

principal surviving monument of Antiphellus is its beautiful and well-preserved Hellenistic theatre, which stands in a superb position above the seashore some 500 m (550 yd) west of the port. Within the town there is also a superb Lycian sarcophagus, which stands in a picturesque little square a short distance above the harbour.

The theatre at Antiphellus.

Between Kaş and Finike, the next port town to the east, 68 km (42 miles) away, there are many ancient Lycian sites; some of them along the shore which should be seen by boat, for this is the most beautiful and fascinating stretch of the Turkish coast, particularly the part around Kekova island.

The major site along this part of the coast is Myra, 37 km (23 miles) east of Kaş, which lies just outside the village of Demre. Those going to the site by sea land at Andriace, the ancient port of Myra, where there is another huge granary built by Hadrian during his tour of Asia Minor in AD 125. Busts of Hadrian and Faustina the Elder can still be seen over the entrance of the building.

MYRA

Lycian tombs at Myra.

The site of ancient Myra is a very dramatic one, with the Lycian acropolis on the lofty ridge of a rocky crag, approached by a stepped path that ascends to the western edge of the citadel. The oldest parts of the walls on the citadel date to the sixth century BC, the earliest extant remains of the Lycian city. The southeast and southwest sides of the precipice are pockmarked with Lycian tombs and strewn with sarcophagi, most of which date from the fourth century BC. Below the citadel, to the southwest, is the splendid theatre, which in its present form dates from the Imperial Roman era.

The tombs at Myra are divided into two groups, those in the cliff-face flanking the theatre, and those on the cliff below the acropolis to the southeast. Most of the tombs are of the house type, modelled on ordinary Lycian dwellings, although a few are temple facades in miniature. Several of the tombs are decorated with elaborate reliefs; the most notable being the Painted Tomb, one of the most striking in all of Lycia, with a scene depicting eleven life-sized figures.

LIMYRA

Thirty-one km (19 miles) beyond Demre one comes to Finike, a port town that occupies the site of ancient Phoenicus, of which not a trace remains. There are a number of Lycian sites in the hinterland north of Finike, most of them situated along the valleys of the two rivers known to the Greeks as the Arycandus and the Limyrus. The nearest of these is Limyra, some 5 km (3 miles) inland. During the first half of the fourth century BC Limyra was the capital of a kingdom ruled by a local warlord named Pericles, whose magnificent tomb was recently discovered on the acropolis of the ancient city. The Tomb of Pericles was decorated with superb reliefs depicting him leading his troops into battle on a chariot; these are now in the Antalya Museum. Another remarkable tomb at Limyra, discovered by Fellows, is dedicated to a nobleman named Catabura, a close relative of King Pericles.

Finike is at the western end of an immense bay that terminates, on its eastern side, at Cape Gelidonya, the southeasternmost promontory in Lycia. Beyond this the coastline turns abruptly north to form the long western side of the Gulf of Antalya. Beyond Finike the highway curves around in a great arc to cut across the base of the Gelidonya peninsula, coming out to the sea again south of Kemer on the Antalya Gulf. Along the latter part of this stretch there are signposted turn-offs for Olympus and Phaselis, the easternmost cities of the ancient Lycian League.

OLYMPUS AND PHASELIS

Olympus took its name from Mount Olympus of Lycia, the peak known in Turkish as Tahtalí Dağ, which rises to a height of 2,365 m (7,800 ft) some 16 km (10 miles) to the north along the coast, almost directly inland from Phaselis. The patron deity of Lycian Olympus was Hephaestus, god of the forge, whose hearth was believed to be the fire that has been burning since antiquity on a mountaintop above the town just to its south; this was also believed to be the fire-breathing Chimaera, the monster killed by Bellerophon in one of his legendary exploits. Olympus is a very romantic site, its unexcavated ruins lying along both sides of a stagnant river that ends in the silted-up port of the ancient city, with the walls of the citadel still evident on the rocky crag that towers over the beach on the left bank. A path leading up from the left bank of the river brings one to the most notable structure in Olympus, the complete cella door of an Ionic temple; an inscription records that this edifice was erected in AD 172–5 and dedicated to the emperor Marcus Aurelius.

Phaselis stands on the seashore directly under Mount Olympus of Lycia, with the heavily overgrown ruins of the city spread out over a boot-shaped peninsula. According to tradition, Phaselis was founded here in 690 BC by Dorian

119

Plan of Phaselis.
1. theatre; 2. south
agora; 3. south
harbour; 4. Gate of
Hadrian; 5. north
harbour; 6. defence
walls; 7. necropolis.

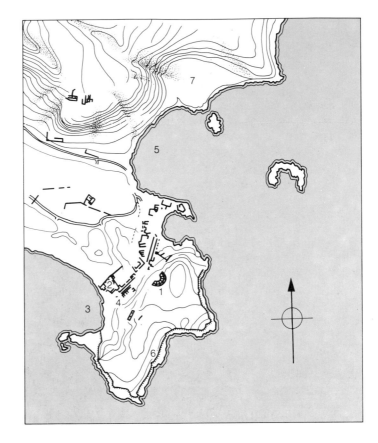

colonists from Rhodes, who were led by an Argive hero
named Lacius. The men of Phaselis were renowned traders,
and theirs was one of the nine cities which together founded
Naucratis, the 'Queen of the Nile'. Otherwise, Phaselis had
much the same history as the other cities of this region in
antiquity, liberated from the Persians by Alexander the
Great in 333 BC, fought over by the Diadochoi, and then
allowed considerable local autonomy under Roman rule as
a member of the Lycian League.

The **theatre** (1) and other structures date from the Imperial
Roman era, with an inscription on the south **agora** (2)
recording that it was dedicated to the emperor Domitian.
Near the **south harbour** (3), a **Gate of Hadrian** (4) has an
inscription recording that it was erected at the time of his visit
to Phaselis in AD 130. Other inscriptions found on the hill

across the avenue from the theatre indicate that two temples stood there: one of them was dedicated to Athena Polias, the patron goddess of Phaselis, and was founded in the fifth century BC; the second was a Temple of Hestia and Hermes, dating from the third century BC.

Archaeologists have recently unearthed an ancient settlement on the heights above the **north harbour** (5), along with remains of the **defence walls** (6) that enclosed it during the Hellenistic period. The **necropolis** (7) of Phaselis was burrowed into this hill, with funerary monuments in the form of structured tombs as well as sepulchres and sarcophagi, one of which now lies on the beach of the north harbour.

Beyond Phaselis the highway heads due north and goes straight up the coast to Antalya, 113 km (70 miles) from Finike. On the left the lofty range of Beydağlarí, the Mountains of the Lord, rises in serried tiers to its highest peak at Mount Climax, at nearly 2,261 m (7,500 ft). Straight ahead, the enormous ramparts of the Taurus rise above the Pamphylian plain, whose seemingly endless sand-fringed shore stretches off toward infinity on the east. As one rounds the end of the bay west of Antalya one passes into Pamphylia, leaving behind the tomb-haunted landscape of Lycia.

The theatre and stage-building at Phaselis.

PAMPHYLIA

Pamphylia was the coastal region bounded on the north by the Taurus Mountains, its western and eastern limits marked by the great cities of Antalya and Alanya. Most of the ancient cities of Pamphylia were on or near the Mediterranean coast, but a few were some distance inland, merging with the cities of Pisidia, the region north of the Pamphylian plain. According to Herodotus and Strabo, the Pamphylians were descended from veterans of Agamemnon's army, a 'mixed multitude' who followed the seers Amphilochus, Calchas and Mopsus in a great migration along the Anatolian coast after the Trojan War.

(*Opposite*) The stage-building of the Roman theatre at Aspendus.

The principal town in Pamphylia today is Antalya, which is magnificently situated at the northwestern corner of the great gulf that bears its name. Antalya is ancient Attaleia, named after Attalus II of Pergamum, who founded the city in 159 BC, the first year of his reign. Attalus intended the city to be the principal Pergamene port on the Mediterranean coast, and enclosed it with a line of powerful defence walls and towers which were re-built in Roman times and still survive in part today. Attaleia was the principal port in Pamphylia throughout antiquity and on into the medieval

ATTALEIA (ANTALYA)

The Pamphylian shore.

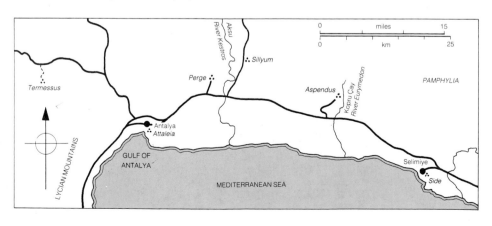

Byzantine era.

The oldest part of Antalya is the quarter around the port, whose monuments include structures from the Hellenistic, Roman, Byzantine, Selcuk and Ottoman periods, as well as some picturesque old Turkish houses. The port quarter is still ringed by some fragmentary remains of the defence walls. The best-preserved stretch of the walls is along Atatürk Caddesi, the main avenue that runs south from the city centre and then curves around to the cliff south of the port. A short way along this avenue on the right one comes to the Gate of Hadrian, the monumental propylon erected to celebrate the Emperor's visit to Attaleia in AD 130. The gateway itself consists of three coffered arches, flanked by two older towers of the Hellenistic walls.

At the seaward end of Atatürk Caddesi is another impressive monument, the huge round tower known as Hídírlík Kulesi. This massive structure, which probably dates from the second century AD, consists of a huge cylindrical drum on a square base, surmounted by a poorly built parapet which was perhaps added later. The tower resembles Hadrian's mausoleum in Rome, better known as the Castel Sant'Angelo, and is believed to have been built as a sepulchre for a local notable.

The Antalya Archaeological Museum is west of the town centre along Konyaaltí Caddesi. This museum has one of the most attractive and interesting displays of any local institution in Turkey; its exhibits span the whole spectrum of

The Gate of Hadrian, Antalya.

civilization in Anatolia, concentrating on the Antalya region, but including Lycia and Pisidia.

To the northwest of Antalya, 25 km (16 miles) away, are the extremely impressive ruins of ancient Termessus. Termessus is perched on a peak of Güllü Dağ, the Rosy Mountain, whose summit is 1,067 m (3,500 ft) above sea-level. The route starts out along the main highway to Burdur and Isparta, turning off after 11 km (7 miles) on to the Korkuteli highway, which passes the approach road to the archaeological site. The new road now brings one to a parking-lot at the base of the acropolis hill; from there a steep path leads up to the ancient city, which is set in a scene of wild beauty at the top of the mountain. Its ruins are completely overgrown with trees and underbrush, with ancient walls and sarcophagi tumbled about in romantic disorder. Although Termessus was within the bounds of the Roman province of Pamphylia, it is actually in Pisidia, close to the eastern bounds of Lycia.

The well-preserved theatre is the most attractive structure in Termessus; it was built in the Hellenistic period and, though rebuilt in Roman times, it retains its original Greek form. Another well-preserved and attractive monument is the bouleuterion, whose walls still stand to a height of 10 m (32½ ft). This dates from the Hellenistic period and combines both Doric and Ionic elements in its design. The handsome stoa just to the northwest of the bouleuterion, beyond the agora,

TERMESSUS

The theatre at Termessus.

was donated to the city by King Attalus II of Pergamum, probably when he founded Attaleia.

There are the remains of seven temples in Termessus, two of them dedicated to Artemis, one to Zeus, and one to the emperor Hadrian, the others unidentified. The principal temple of Termessus was a Doric Temple of Artemis; this is an edifice of the Antonine period (AD 138–92) with six by nine columns; one of its reliefs shows the goddess in the sacrificial scenes from *Iphigenia in Aulis*, the tragedy by Euripides. The second Temple of Artemis is a small but well-preserved temple with a front porch but no peripteral colonnade, dating from the Imperial Roman era. The Temple of Zeus is a small structure consisting of just a cella without columns. This was dedicated to Zeus Solymeus, representing the syncreti-zation of Zeus and a mountain deity of the Solymoi. The Temple of Hadrian is a peripteros of the Ionic order, totally ruined except for its perfectly preserved Roman entryway. The other three temples are all small edifices of the Corin-thian order.

One very interesting structure south of the Stoa of Attalus is known as the Founder's House. This is a Roman mansion built around an unroofed atrium, with its splendid Doric portal still standing to a height of 6 m (20 ft). The house takes its name from an inscription at the entrance, which records that the owner was 'Founder of the City', referring to his civic benefactions in Termessus.

Termessus is surrounded on all sides except the east by its vast necropolis, with rock-cut tombs, built tombs and sarco-phagi covering the slopes of the mountainside, all of them of the Lycian type. The most impressive of these has been identified as the Tomb of Alcetas, one of Alexander's generals who was killed here in 319 BC by Antigonus, during the wars of the Diadochoi.

PERGE

From Antalya the main highway runs through the heart of the Pamphylian plain all the way to Alanya, a distance of 84 km (52 miles). Some 13 km (8 miles) east of Antalya there is an approach road on the left leading to Perge, one of the most important cities of ancient Pamphylia.

Like Termessus, Perge's first appearance in history came in 333 BC, when the city surrendered to Alexander after the Macedonians marched into Pamphylia. The city is renowned as the birthplace of Apollonius of Perge, one of the greatest mathematicians of the Hellenistic age, who was born here *c*. 260 BC. It was also famous for its shrine of Artemis Pergaea, which the orator Polemo, speaking in the time of Hadrian, praised as a 'marvel of size, beauty, and workmanship'. Despite its fame, no trace has ever been found of this shrine, though Turkish archaeologists continue to excavate for it.

The road to the archaeological site brings one first to the theatre and the stadium, which are just outside the outer gate of the ancient city on the left. The theatre was built in the Hellenistic period and reconstructed in the Imperial Roman era, with a seating capacity of 14,000. The stage-building is still largely intact.

Within the stage-building there are interesting reliefs from the life of Dionysus, the god of the theatre as well as of the vine, wine and religious ecstasy. One of the reliefs depicts the birth of Dionysus, the son of Zeus and Semele. Another scene shows Dionysus with Artemis Pergaea, who initiated him into the rites of her cult and taught him the cultivation of the vine. A third relief portrays a Dionysian procession, in which Dionysus is carried in a chariot drawn by two panthers and bedecked with vine leaves and ivy, accompanied by a Bacchante and a Satyr.

The stadium, which seated some 12,000 spectators, is the best preserved in Asia Minor after that at Aphrodisias. It was probably erected in the second century AD, with an arena measuring 34 × 234 m (111 × 767 ft).

Just to the right of the outer gate are the remains of a funerary monument erected late in Hadrian's reign; this is identified by an inscription as a memorial to a wealthy lady named Plancia Magna, whose name appears in a score of places elsewhere in Perge as a benefactress. The main gate and the walls that stretch off from it on either side were built in the fourth century AD, after Perge had expanded beyond its original walls, which enclosed a smaller area under the flat-topped acropolis-hill to the north. The shattered round towers of the original Hellenistic gate can be seen framed in the portal of the late Roman gate as one approaches the entrance to the city. The inner and outer gateways were connected by curtain walls, with the east wall ending at the agora. During the reign of Septimius Severus (AD 193–211) a nymphaeum and a propylon were built into the west curtain wall, with the latter leading into the Roman baths of the city.

The remains of the inner gateway of Perge seen through the outer gateway.

On the right, between the agora and the outer gateway, are the remains of an apsidal structure that served as a church in the early Byzantine period.

The inner gateway, with its two splendid round towers built of ashlar masonry, is all that remains of the original ring walls of the Hellenistic city. Inside the gateway is a magnificent courtyard of horseshoe shape, from which one entered the inner city via a two-storeyed gateway with three portals, a structure that Plancia Magna built for Perge in AD 120–2. Niches and pedestals around the periphery of this courtyard supported statues of Roman emperors and empresses and of the city's founders.

The courtyard within the inner gateway opens onto the beginning of a colonnaded way that was the main thoroughfare of the ancient city; its marble paving still shows the ruts of wagon-wheels. The street is divided by a water-channel with a series of cascading pools, fed by the nymphaeum at its upper end. The street was flanked by statues and its sidewalks opened onto arcaded shops. There were also shops in the outer arcade of the agora, a large market-place 65 m (213 ft) square, built in the fourth century AD, probably at the same time as the outer walls. This street and the one that crossed it near its upper end divided the city into two pairs of unequal quarters. Within the southwestern corner are the remains of an apsidal basilica that served as the bishopric of Byzantine Perge; and on the lower side of the quarter above it is a palaestra dedicated to the emperor Claudius by a citizen named C. Julius Cornutus. The ruins on the acropolis-hill above the city on its north side are all from the Byzantine period, built on the foundations of the original prehistoric settlement founded by the 'mixed multitudes' after the fall of Troy.

SILLYUM

About 3 km (2 miles) past the Perge turn-off is a road to the left leading to Sillyum, which is 5 km (3 miles) north as the eagle flies, but much longer on the meandering country road. Despite its proximity to the main highway, Sillyum is seldom visited, so that its ruins still have that romantic appeal which many of the more famous sites lost only two decades ago. The ruins of the ancient city are on the flat top of the acropolis-hill, which is 213.5 m (700 ft) high, rising above the hamlet of Asar Köyü.

Sillyum is as old as Perge, and it too had the tradition of being established by the 'mixed multitudes'. The most interesting remnant there, other than the picturesque ruins themselves, is a door-jamb covered with a lengthy inscription; dated c. 200 BC, this is the principal evidence for the ancient Pamphylian language, which was written in Greek letters, but as yet remains little understood.

ASPENDUS

Sixteen kilometres (10 miles) beyond the Sillyum road is a turning for Aspendus. The ancient site is 4 km (2½ miles) up the fertile valley of the Köprü Çay, known to the Greeks as the Eurymedon.

Archaeological evidence has in general confirmed that the city's acropolis-hill was occupied as early as the late Bronze Age, with a second wave of settlers arriving during the dark ages of the Hellenic world. Inscriptions indicate that the later settlers were Greeks from Arcadia.

The road to the archaeological site leads directly to the Roman theatre at Aspendus, the most magnificent edifice of its type that has survived from the classical world. The theatre was built by the architect Zenon during the reign of Marcus Aurelius, and inscriptions in Greek and Latin over the entrances to the stage-building record that it was a gift of two brothers, Curtius Crispinus and Curtius Auspicatus, who dedicated it 'to the gods of the country and to the Imperial House'.

One can appreciate here better than anywhere else in Asia Minor the total effect of a Roman theatre, particularly since the structure is so remarkably well preserved. The theatre is directly under the east side of the acropolis-hill, where most of the other buildings of the city stand. The auditorium rests in part against the east slope of the hillside, but most of the edifice stands almost entirely on barrel-vaulted substructures. The stage-building is an imposing structure — some 25 m (82 ft) high and 110 m (369 ft) wide across its outer facade — with the five major tiers of its windows corresponding to the different levels of the interior. The tower-like entrance is not an original part of the structure, but was erected by the Selcuk Turks early in the 13th century, when Sultan Alaeddin Keykubad I used the stage-building as his palace.

The interior of the theatre is almost as well preserved as its exterior, lacking only the columns and other architectural elements and sculptures that once adorned the inner facade of the stage-building. The stage-building consisted of a facade, and a proscenium, the colonnaded platform on

The theatre at Aspendus.

which the play was performed. The facade extended for two storeys above the proscenium; the uppermost storey was used principally to support an awning-like roof that projected over the stage to improve the acoustics. The two lower levels of the façade were adorned with a double arcade of ten columns each, complete with their entablature, with the lower colonnade Ionic and the upper one Corinthian. The central quartet of columns on the upper level was surmounted by a pediment with a relief of Dionysus; the other panels depicted scenes in relief and also supported statues and portrait busts.

The auditorium extends somewhat beyond the usual semi-circle of a Roman theatre. The parodoi, which in Greek theatres were always open and approached the orchestra at an angle, are here parallel to the front of the semicircular orchestra and covered with a barrel vault. The auditorium was designed to seat somewhat less than 20,000. The seats are divided horizontally by a single diazoma, with 20 tiers of seats below and 21 above it. Ten radial stairways rise from the orchestra to the diazoma, and 21 more stairways ascend to the uppermost tier, which is backed by an arcaded gallery with 59 vaults. Special seats in the front row were reserved for high-ranking officials such as senators and magistrates; the priestesses of Vesta sat in private boxes in the two tower-like structures that flank the stage-building.

The stadium is below the east flank of the acropolis-hill to the north of the theatre. This immense structure is 30 m (96 ft) wide and 215 m (705 ft) long, and though it is overgrown with grass its outline is clearly discernable. There are two rock-hewn tombs near the stadium, the most impressive being the one just to its east. Beyond this are a number of sarcophagi, all part of the necropolis of Aspendus.

There were three approaches to the acropolis in antiquity, two of them leading up via declivities on the north and south sides of the hill directly behind the theatre, and the third on the north side of the main acropolis-hill. The most convenient approach from the theatre today is via the north gate, where the path brings one up to what was once the civic centre of Aspendus. Here one sees the impressive remains of the bouleuterion, a market hall with arcaded shops, a basilica and a nymphaeum, as well as the ruins of an unidentified building just inside the south gate.

The south gate is the best vantage-point from which to

The Roman aqueduct
at Aspendus.

view the great Roman aqueduct of Aspendus, the best-preserved in Asia Minor. This round-arched structure brought water into the city from the mountains to the north, conducting it across the intervening valley and up to the northeast slope of the acropolis hill, making a sharp bend in the process. At two points, the first at the foot of the mountain, and the second about 100 m (324 ft) from the acropolis, the original head of pressure forced the water up into open-topped towers some 30 m (96 ft) high, carried on superimposed arches, from which it descended on the other side. These water-control towers are the most striking features of this magnificent aqueduct, which gives a grand and Roman look to the whole valley between the ancient city and the mountains to its north.

SIDE

Twenty-five kilometres (16 miles) past the Aspendus road is a turning for Selimiye, the site of ancient Side, which is on the sea some 4 km (2½ miles) distant. Along the approach to Selimiye one can see stretches of the Roman aqueduct that carried water 24 km (15 miles) from the foothills of the Taurus Mountains to Side, whose outlying ruins lie scattered in the fields on both sides of the road. Then the road finally brings one through the outer defence walls beside what was once the **main gateway** (1) to ancient Side.

According to Strabo, Side was founded by settlers from the Aeolian city of Cyme; modern scholarship dates the colony to *c*. 750 BC. Strabo also writes that a slave-market was established here by the infamous pirates of Cilicia.

Side is still ringed by its ancient defence walls, which sealed off the peninsula on which the city was founded. These exceptionally well-built structures are among the finest examples of Hellenistic fortifications on the southern coast of Turkey, and probably date from the second century BC. The main entrance through the fortifications, which is near the northern end of the land walls that enclose the city on its eastern side, is a double gateway, with an outer and inner portal flanked by two massive towers.

Inside the main gate the road continues along what was once one of the main streets of Side, a **colonnaded way** (2) that led to the **agora** (3), the **theatre** (4), the **baths** (5) and other public buildings at the city centre. Some of the columns that once lined this avenue have in recent years been re-erected by the Turkish archaeologists who have been excavating the site. At the western end of the colonnaded way one comes to the main square of ancient Side, with the agora and the theatre on the left, the gate to the inner city straight ahead, and one of the Roman baths on the right. The

City plan of Side.
1. main gateway;
2. colonnaded way;
3. agora; 4. theatre;
5. baths;
6. Byzantine basilica;
7. state agora;
8. monumental gate;
9. Temple of Dionysus; 10. Roman baths; 11. Byzantine fountain; 12. temple;
13. basilica;
14. Temple of Apollo.

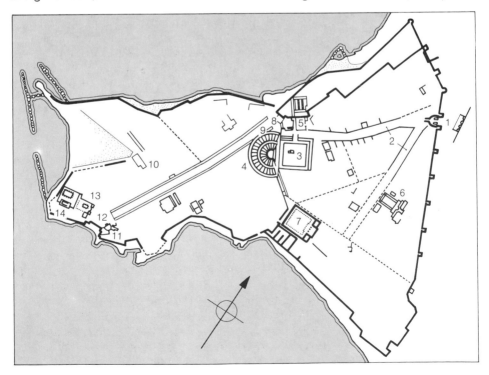

133

baths, which date from the fifth century AD, have now been restored and are used to exhibit antiquities discovered in the excavations at Side, which include some of the finest Roman statuary in Asia Minor.

The propylon of the agora was directly across the avenue from the baths. This led into a vast market-square, measuring 91 × 94 m (298 × 306 ft), surrounded on all four sides by stoas which date from the second century AD. The round structure near the centre of the square has been identified as the foundation of a shrine dedicated to Tyche, the goddess of fortune, known to the Romans as Fortuna.

At some time in the mid-fourth century AD another fortification wall was built across the neck of the peninsula, after which the people of Side withdrew to the inner city on the tip of the peninsula for defence against the onslaughts of the Goths. But apparently the outer city was not abandoned altogether, for some 200 m (220 yd) southeast of the agora there stands a large **Byzantine basilica** (6) which dates from the fifth or sixth century. The part of town in which the basilica stands must have been where the working people of Side lived, because it was known as the Quarter of the Guilds.

The inner defence wall included the theatre in its line of fortifications, with its southern extension running from the corner of the auditorium on that side down to the inner stoa and another great colonnaded square near the sea, where the walls extended westward along the beach as far as the city's fortified harbour. The latter square has been identified as the **state agora** (7), a huge area that measures 69.2 × 88.5 m (204 × 290 ft), surrounded on all sides by Ionic stoas some 7 m (23 ft) in width. On its eastern side are the remains of a complex of three large chambers; the two on the sides possibly served as a library and archives, and the central one was reserved for the use of the Emperor.

Detail of a Hellenistic sarcophagus in the museum near the theatre at Side.

The theatre is by far the most important and impressive monument in Side, and is an extremely evocative sight when viewed against the background of the sand dunes that have half-buried the ruined city on its southern side. It was constructed in the second century AD and is thus Roman in design, but the architect retained one essentially Greek feature, in that he extended the arc of the auditorium beyond a semicircle by 30 degrees on either side of its diameter. Consequently, the vaulted passages of the paradoi make that same angle with the proscenium.

The stage-building must have been splendidly adorned, as one can see from the fragmentary architectural structures and reliefs that tumbled into the orchestra in some great earthquake in times past. During the late Roman period a wall was constructed at the front of the orchestra to protect spectators during gladiatorial combats and fights involving wild animals. Inscriptions and poorly preserved frescoes reveal that the theatre was converted into an open-air church in the fifth or sixth century.

The theatre at Side, with the agora and Roman baths in the background.

The **monumental gate** (8) to the inner city lies just to the right of the theatre, and now serves as the entrance to Selimiye village. The gate was once surmounted by an architrave and attic, on top of which was probably a quadriga, as evidenced by the fact that the surrounding neighbourhood was known as the Quarter of the Quadriga. Just to the left of the gate, as one approaches it from the outer city, is a recently restored fountain-house dedicated to Vespasian. Just inside the gate on the left are the remains of a small pseudo-peripteral temple, that is, one with half-columns set against the cella walls rather than a true peripteral colonnade of free-standing columns. Its proximity to the theatre has led to its identification as a **Temple of Dionysus** (9).

Another colonnaded avenue began just inside the inner gate, and extended diagonally southwestward to the tip of the peninsula. This avenue is now the main street of Selimiye village, which means that much of the inner city of ancient Side cannot be excavated. About 400 m (440 yd) along the avenue, a side street on the right leads to the little port of Selimiye, which is on the silted-up harbour of the ancient city. Continuing along the ancient avenue, one passes on the left the unexcavated remains of a large **Roman baths** (10). The road then peters out at the easternmost end of the peninsula, where there are the remains of five ancient structures. Two of these structures are on the beach just to the left of where the avenue ends; one of them has been identified as a **Byzantine fountain** (11) and the other as a tiny **temple** (12) dedicated to the Anatolian god Men, dated to the second century AD.

The other three structures form a complex out on the promontory that once formed the southern arm of Side's harbour. The innermost of the three structures is a large **basilica** (13), whose forecourt included the ruins of the two structures immediately to its west. These are almost identical Corinthian hexastyle peripteral temples, with six columns in front, dating from the latter part of the second century AD; the one on the left is dedicated to Apollo and that on the right to Artemis. Some of the columns of the **Temple of Apollo** (14) have recently been re-erected, making this perhaps the most romantic sight along the whole of the Turkish coast, particularly when the colonnade is seen against the background of a Pamphylian sunset.

POSTSCRIPT

Side seems the last outpost of ancient classical civilization as one proceeds eastward along the Mediterranean coast of Turkey, passing from Pamphylia to Cilicia at Alanya. But there are a number of other classical sites of some importance along Turkey's southern coast as well as in the interior of Anatolia, for Graeco-Roman civilization spread throughout the subcontinent. Calder and Bean's *Classical Atlas of Asia Minor* maps the sites of 1,382 ancient Greek cites in Anatolia, some of them with major monuments still standing, others with just a few scattered stones lying half-buried in the earth or built into the walls of a local village that may perpetuate the ancient name ot an historic *polis*. Listed here are a few of the most outstanding of these classical sites that lie beyond the range of the itineraries followed in the previous chapters.

CILICIA

The most important classical sites in Cilicia can be reached from the coastal city of Silifke, the ancient Seleucia-ad-Calycadnum, founded at the beginning of the third century BC by Seleucus I. One site is at Uzuncaburç, some 30 km (19 miles) north of Silifke, where one finds the ruins of the ancient Phrygian city of Olba, which from the time of Vespasian onwards was known as Diocaesarea. The principal monument of Olba-Diocaesarea is the exceptionally well-preserved Temple of Zeus Olbius. This was erected by Seleucus I at the beginning of the third century BC, and is the earliest-known temple built in the Corinthian order.

There are three sites along the coast between Silifke and Mersin, 115 km (71 miles) to the east. The first of these is Corycius, 21 km (13 miles) east of Silifke, whose ruins lie along the shore at Kíz Kalesi, the Maiden's Castle, named after the romantic sea-girt fortress just offshore from the ruins of the ancient city. Some 13 km (8 miles) beyond that there is a turn-off for Kanytelis, the site of ancient Elaeusa-Sebaste. The third site is at Viranşehir, 11 km (7 miles) west of Mersin, where one finds the site of ancient Soli-Pompeiopolis.

PHRYGIA

Composite capital in the Temple of Zeus, Aezani.

The region east of Lydia in west-central Anatolia was known in antiquity as Phrygia. The capital of Phrygia in the archaic period was Gordion, some 75 km (47 miles) southwest of Ankara, where excavations have uncovered the royal tomb of the Phrygian kings, the most famous of whom was Midas. The principal classical monument in Phrygia is at Çavdarhisar, a village 24 km (15 miles) southwest of Kütahya. This is the site of Aezani, an ancient Phrygian town that flourished under Roman rule. The only monument of Aezani that has survived is the magnificent Temple of Zeus; this was one of the best-preserved Roman temples in Anatolia until it was severely damaged by an earthquake in 1970, but it is now being restored. The capitals in the front and rear porches are among the most remarkable in Asia Minor: they combine the Ionic volute with the Corinthian acanthus and are of the type known as Composite, which emerged in the early Roman Imperial era.

GALATIA

The oldest Roman temple in Anatolia is in Ankara, the modern capital of Turkey, which in antiquity was the Galatian city of Ancyra. This edifice was probably built in the years 25-30 BC, just after the annexation of Galatia by Augustus, and was dedicated to the newly instituted cult of Augustus and Rome. The temple is still impressive despite its ruined state.

COMMAGENE

The most remote classical site in Anatolia is on Nemrut Dağ, a peak some 250 km (155 miles) northeast of Gaziantep. This is the site of the extraordinary mountain-top tomb-sanctuary of King Antiochus of Commagene, who was assassinated in 96 BC. (Commagene was the last independent kingdom in Asia Minor until its annexation by Vespasian in AD 72.) The monument is an enormous tumulus surmounted by colossal statues of the royal ancestors of Antiochus, the heads of which have long since been toppled to the ground. This is one of the most stirring sights in Turkey, all the more remarkable for its remoteness from the Aegean shore, where the Greeks founded their first cities in this subcontinent of Asia a thousand years before the fall of Commagene.

CHRONOLOGY

BRONZE AGE (*c.* 3,000–1,200 BC)

c. 3,000–2,500	Troy I; first settlement at Old Smyrna
c. 1,500	First settlement at Miletus
c. 1,300–1,260	Troy VII, the Homeric city
c. 1,260	Fall of Troy
c. 1,200	Fall of Mycenae

ANATOLIAN DARK AGES (*c.* 1,200–*c.* 750 BC)

c. 1,200–1,100	Settlement of 'mixed multitudes' in Pamphylia and Cilicia
c. 1,050–900	Migration of Aeolian, Ionian and Dorian Greeks to Aegean coast of Anatolia and offshore islands
c. 950–900	First Greek settlement at Smyrna
c. 900–700	Rise of Phrygian, Lydian, Carian and Lycian cultures in western Anatolia
c. 800	Foundation of Aeolian, Ionian and Dorian Leagues
757	Aeolian Cyme establishes first Asian Greek colony in Magna Graecia at Cumae

ARCHAIC PERIOD (*c.* 750–479 BC)

c. 750–700	Beginnings of Greek literature with epics of Homer
750–600	Ionian cities establish colonies throughout the Mediterranean and in the Hellespont, Propontis and Euxine
700–650	Aeolian temple built at Neandria
c. 665	King Gyges of Lydia invades Ionia
c. 650	Construction of Temple of Athena at Assos
c. 640	Construction of Temple of Athena at Smyrna
c. 600	King Alyattes of Lydia destroys Smyrna
600–500	Beginnings of Greek lyric poetry, science and philosophy in Ionia
561–546	Reign of King Croesus of Lydia
560–550	Building of the archaic Artemisium at Ephesus, and the archaic Temple of Apollo at Didmya
546	Croesus defeated by Cyrus the Great; Greek cities in Anatolia subjugated by Persia
499	Ionian cities revolt against Persia and burn Sardis
494	Persians crush Ionian revolt and destroy Miletus
490	Persians invade Greece and are defeated at Marathon

139

c. 484	Herodotus born at Halicarnassus
480	Persian King Xerxes invades Greece and is defeated at Salamis
479	Persians defeated at Plataea and Mycale; Xerxes destroys Miletus and Didyma

CLASSICAL PERIOD (479–323 BC)

478–c. 468	Delian Confederacy formed
late 5th C	Construction of Nereid Monument at Xanthus
377–353	Mausolus rules in Caria; begins Mausoleum at Halicarnassus and Temple of Zeus at Labraynda
358	Founding of Letoum in Caria
356	Birth of Alexander the Great; archaic Artemisium at Ephesus destroyed by fire; 'later Artemisium' begun soon afterwards
mid–4th C	Construction of Temple of Aphrodite at Cnidus
340	Construction of Temple of Athena at Priene
336	Accession of Alexander
334–333	Alexander conquers Asia Minor at the beginning of his invasion of Asia
323	Death of Alexander

HELLENISTIC PERIOD (323–130 BC)

323–302	Age of the Diadochoi, Alexander's successors; Antigonus rules in western Asia Minor
312	Seleucus seizes Babylon and founds Seleucid dynasty
306	Lysimachus begins rule in Thrace
302	Antigonus defeated and killed at battle of Ipsus by Lysimachus and Seleucus; Lysimachus extends kingdom into Asia Minor
c. 300	Rebuilding of Temple of Apollo at Didyma begins
early 3rd C	Beginning of first phase of Temple of Artemis at Sardis; construction of Temple of Zeus at Olba-Diocaesarea
281	Lysimachus defeated and killed at battle of Corupedium by Seleucus, who extends rule into Asia Minor; Seleucus assassinated and succeeded by Antiochus; Philetaerus gains control of Pergamum
281–263	Philetaerus reigns at Pergamum; builds Temples of Athena and Demeter
263–241	Eumenes I reigns in Pergamum, beginning Attalid dynasty
241–197	Attalus I reigns in Pergamum
230	Attalus I defeats Gauls and forms alliance with Rome
223–187	Antiochus III rules over Seleucid Empire
First half of 2nd C	Construction of Temple of Dionysus at Teos and of Temple of Artemis at Magnesia-ad-Maeandrum

197–159	Eumenes II reigns in Pergamum; builds library and Altar of Zeus, rebuilds theatre
190	Eumenes II defeats Gauls
189	Eumenes II and Roman allies defeat Antiochus III at battle of Magnesia
188	Treaty of Apamea ends Seleucid rule in Asia Minor
159–138	Attalus II reigns in Pergamum; builds Temple of Hera
138–133	Attalus III reigns in Pergamum
133	Attalus III dies and bequeaths his kingdom to Rome

ROMAN PERIOD (129 BC–AD 330)

129	Organization of Roman Province of Asia Minor
27	Octavian becomes Augustus
last quarter of 1st C	Construction of Temple of Augustus and Roma at Ancyra; first phase of Temple of Aphrodite at Aphrodisias

AD

14	Death of Augustus
14–37	Reign of Tiberius
44–56	Missionary journeys of St. Paul; founding of first Christian churches in Asia Minor
54–68	Reign of Nero
69–79	Reign of Vespasian
81–96	Reign of Domitian; construction of Temple of Domitian at Ephesus
98–117	Reign of Trajan; Trajaneum begun at Pergamum; Library of Celsus built at Ephesus
first half of 2nd C	Construction of Temple of Zeus at Euromus
117–38	Reign of Hadrian; Trajaneum completed at Pergamum; Temple of Hadrian built at Ephesus; completion of Temple of Aphrodite at Aphrodisias; Temple of Zeus built at Aezani; construction of Temple of Hadrian at Cyzicus
138–61	Reign of Antoninus Pius; last phase of Temple of Artemis at Sardis
161–80	Reign of Marcus Aurelius; theatre built at Aspendus
last half of 2nd C	Temples of Apollo and Artemis erected at Side
193–211	Reign of Septimius Severus
211–17	Reign of Caracalla; construction of Temple of Dionysus at Pergamum
263–70	Goths invade Asia Minor
285–305	Reign of Diocletian
324	Constantine becomes sole ruler of Roman Empire; begins to build new capital at Byzantium on the Bosphorus

BYZANTINE PERIOD (330–1453)

330	Constantinople (formerly Byzantium) becomes capital of the Roman Empire (whose eastern regions later came to be called the Byzantine Empire)
330–37	Constantine the Great reigns in Constantinople
392	Edict of Theodosius I banning paganism
401	Destruction of Artemisium by Christians
524–65	Reign of Justinian the Great; zenith of Byzantine power
616	Ephesus, Sardis and other cities in western Asia Minor destroyed by Persians under Chosroes II

A note on ancient sources

A number of ancient sources have been referred to in this book, beginning with Homer (*fl.* second half of the eighth century BC) and Herodotus (*c*. 484 BC- before 420 BC), both of whom were eastern Greeks. Two other important sources are Strabo and Pausanius. Strabo, (64/63 BC–AD 21 at the latest), a Greek of partly Asian descent, was born at Amasya in Asia Minor and spent much of his life in Rome. His *Geography* in 17 volumes survives in its entirety and is the principal source for the geography of the ancient world, as well as for information about the classical monuments of Asia Minor. Pausanius was also an Asian Greek, probably from Lydia. His *Description of Greece*, written in the mid-second century AD, is the principal source of information about the religious shrines of the Greek world, including those in Asia Minor.

Vitruvius (*fl.* first century BC) was a Roman architect and military engineer whose *De architectura*, (*The Ten Books of Architecture*), is the oldest extant work on architecture and city-planning, incorporating the writings of early Greek architects whose treatises would otherwise have been lost.

NOTE ON CLASSICAL ARCHITECTURE

Classical architecture has a highly technical vocabulary that is explained here with reference to diagrams of archetypical Greek temples and drawings of the two major orders of ancient Greek architecture, the Doric and the Ionic.

The term *cella* is used to denote either the central structure of a temple aside from its surrounding colonnade, or, more specifically, its principal chamber. An inner sanctum within the cella is called a *naiskos*; this structure sheltered the cult-statue of the deity. Many temples have an altar in front of them, which usually faces east, except in sanctuaries of Artemis-Cybele, which always face west.

The front porch of a temple is called the *pronaos*, and the rear porch the *opisthodomus*. Both of those porches are always open, and their side walls terminate in pilasters called *antae*. The columns of these porches are sometimes between the antae, in which case they are said to be *in antis* (a temple whose only columns are between its antae is sometimes called a *templum-in-antis*). The term prostyle can be applied to a temple if its only external columns are in front of its porch; if it has only a pair of columns between the *antae* it is called distyle; if it has four columns at its end it is tetrastyle; if it has six it is hexastyle, etc. If a temple has a surrounding colonnade, the *pteron* or peristyle, it is called a *peripteros*. A temple surrounded by a double colonnade is *dipteral* and a *pseudo-dipteral* temple is one with an outer colonnade placed as if it were dipteral, but with the inner colonnade missing. The prefix 'amphi' means that the temple has the same arrangement of columns at its front and back.

Beginning at its foundations, the principal structures at the base of a temple, which together are called the *crepidoma*, are the *euthynteria*, or levelling course, and the steps (usually three), the topmost one being the *stylobate*, or temple platform.

Doric columns stand directly on the stylobate, whereas Ionic columns rise from a base with very elaborate mouldings. The columns in both orders are fluted, 20 shallow ones in the Doric, 24 deeper ones in the Ionic. Doric capitals surmount the column through an *echinus*, a convex moulding that curves out from the top of the uppermost column drum; above this is the *abacus*, a flat rectangular slab. Ionic capitals are much more elaborate, with characteristic volutes and elaborately carved moulding, known as 'egg and dart' (see the illustration on p. 7).

The horizontal elements above the columns and their capitals together form the entablature. Surmounting the capitals is the architrave or epistyle; in the Doric order this consists of a plain

143

block; in the Ionic order there are three slightly overlapping slabs. Above the architrave is the frieze, or horizontal zone, which in the Doric order is divided into tri-striated *triglyphs* and plane-surfaced *metopes*; this is surmounted by the cornice, which forms the base for the triangular pediment. The frieze was decorated with sculpture; in the Ionic order this was a continuous series of reliefs, but in the Doric order the reliefs were confined to the metopes.

Above the entablature at the ends of the temple are the pediments. The *tympanum*, or triangular wall within the pediment, is usually decorated with sculpture in the Doric order, but this is rarely done in the Ionic order. Statues called *acroteria* stood on the summit and corners of the pediments in Doric temples. In Ionic temples the rain-gutter was often decorated with lion-heads.

The Greek orders of architecture (*top*); parts of a Greek temple (*bottom*).

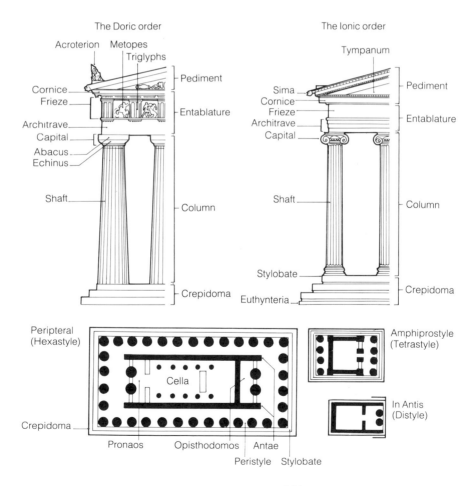

The Doric order

The Ionic order

Acroterion Metopes
Triglyphs
Pediment
Cornice
Frieze
Entablature
Architrave
Capital
Abacus
Echinus
Shaft
Column
Crepidoma

Tympanum
Sima
Cornice
Frieze
Architrave
Capital
Shaft
Column
Stylobate
Euthynteria
Crepidoma
Pediment
Entablature

Peripteral
(Hexastyle)
Cella
Crepidoma
Pronaos   Opisthodomos   Antae
Peristyle   Stylobate

Amphiprostyle
(Tetrastyle)

In Antis
(Distyle)

ARCHITECTURAL GLOSSARY

Aeolic palm-leaf capital developed by the Aeolian Greeks.

Amazonomachy a mythical battle in which the Greeks defeated the Amazons, a favourite theme in Greek sculpture.

Amphitheatre a theatre with an auditorium of circular or oval form surrounding an open arena; used in the Roman world for gladiatorial combats, etc.

Anta (pl. antae) the slightly projecting pilaster of a cella wall.

Architrave a lintel carried from the top of one column to another, the lowest element of an entablature.

Atrium the entrance court of a Roman house, roofed over around its periphery but open at the centre.

Bouleuterion the council house of a Greek city.

Cavea the auditorium of a Greek theatre, the seats of which were usually excavated out of a hillside.

Cella the enclosed central chamber of a Greek temple, also called the naos.

Chryselaphantine a statue with a wooden core overlaid with gold and ivory.

Colonnade a row of columns supporting an entablature.

Composite Corinthian capital combined with Ionic ovolo and volutes.

Corinthian an order differing from the Ionic principally in its capital, which is decorated with volutes and acanthus leaves.

Cornice the upper member of the entablature.

Crepidoma the stepped platform of a Greek temple.

Cunei the sectors into which the seats of a theatre are divided by its aisles.

Diazoma (pl. diazomata) circumferential passageway separating tiers of seats in a theatre.

Dipteral a temple surrounded by a double peristyle.

Dipteros a dipteral temple.

Doric the order originally evolved by the Dorian Greeks.

Drum one of the cylindrical sections of a column shaft.

Echinus the roundel which supports the abacus of a Doric capital; also the similar moulding carved with egg-and-tongue under the cushion of the Ionic capital and between the volutes.

Entablature the superstructure carried by a colonnade, comprising architrave, frieze and cornice.

Euthynteria the top course of a foundation used as a levelling course.

Frieze the middle element of an entablature; also any horizontal zone adorned with reliefs.

Gymnasium a school and athletic centre.

Heroum shrine dedicated to a hero

Intercolumniation the distance between the columns of a colonnade.

Ionic the order developed by the Ionians of the Greek cities in Asia Minor.

Megaron the principal hall of a Mycenaean palace.

Metopes the recessed panels between the triglyphs in a Doric frieze.

Naiskos a small shrine-building, usually the perpetuation of an older sanctuary within a later temple on the same site.

Nymphaeum a monumental fountain considered sacred to the nymphs.

Odeum a roofed building in which rehearsals and musical competitions took place; sometimes used for meetings of the town council.

Opisthodomus the recessed porch in the rear of a Greek temple; sometimes enclosed with bronze grilles and used as a treasury.

Orchestra the space used by the chorus and at first by the actors in the Greek theatre; circular in plan in classical theatres, but generally reduced to a horseshoe in Hellenistic theatres.

Order in ancient Greek architecture this usually consisted of a column with base, shaft and capital, the whole supporting an entablature.

Palaestra a training school, smaller than a *gymnasium*, for physical exercises such as wrestling; usually consisting of a practice ground surrounded by rooms or walls.

Parascenium one of the symmetrical wings of the stage-building which projected into the orchestra

Parodos (*pl.* **parodoi**) side-entrance to the orchestra of a theatre.

Pediment the triangular termination of a ridge roof.

Peripteral a temple whose cella is surrounded by a colonnade.

Peristyle a covered colonnade which surrounds a building, or an inner court with a colonnade.

Plinth a square block forming the bottom of an Ionic base.

Podium a low wall or continuous pedestal on which columns or even entire temples or other monuments are carried.

Portico a colonnaded space, with a roof supported on at least one side by columns.

Pronaos the porch in front of the naos or cella of a temple.

Propylon (*pl.* **propylaea**) the monumental gateway to a city or to the temenos of a temple.

Proscenium a colonnade between the orchestra and the stage-building.

Prostyle a temple with a portico of columns in front.

Prytaneum the town hall in a Greek city.

Pseudo-dipteral a dipteral temple with the inner row of columns omitted.

Pteron a row of columns surrounding a Greek temple.

Quadriga the ancient four-horsed chariot.

Skene the stage-building which formed the back scene of the theatre.

Shaft the main body of a column or pier, between the base and capital.

Stadium running-track where all athletic contests were held.

Stoa (colonnade or portico) a long covered hall with columns in front.

Stylobate the upper step of a temple, which formed a platform for the columns.

Temenos the sacred enclosure or precincts of a temple.

Triglyph a projecting member separating the metopes.

Volute the spiral scroll of the Ionic capital.

Xoanon a primitive wooden icon that served as a cult-figure in a temple.

SELECT BIBLIOGRAPHY

Akurgal, Ekrem, *Ancient Civilizations and Ruins of Turkey*, Istanbul, 1985

Bean, George E., *Aegean Turkey*, London, 1966; *Turkey's Southern Shore*, London, 1968; *Turkey Beyond the Maeander*, London, 1973; *Lycian Turkey*, London, 1978

Blegen, Carl W., *Troy and the Trojans*, London, 1963

Boardman, J., *The Greeks Overseas*, Baltimore, 1964

Burn, A. R., *The Pelican History of Greece*, Harmondsworth, 1966

Calder, W. M. and Bean, George E., *A Classical Map of Asia Minor*, London, 1958

Cahen, Claude, *Pre-Ottoman Turkey*, New York, 1968

Cary, M., *The Greek World from 323–146 BC*, London, 1963

Chandler, Richard, *Travels in Asia Minor*, 1764–1765, reprinted London, 1971

Cook, B. C. *Greek and Roman Art in the British Museum*, London, 1976

Cook, John M., *The Greeks in Ionia and the East*, London, 1962

Dinsmoor, William Bell, *The Architecture of Ancient Greece*, London, 1902

Erim, Kenan T., *Aphrodisias: City of Venus Aphrodite*, London, 1986

Fellows, Charles, *An Account of Discoveries in Lycia*, London, 1841; *Travels and Researches in Asia Minor*, London, 1852

Freely, John, *The Companion Guide to Turkey*, London, 1979; *The Western Shores of Turkey*, London, 1988

Hansen, Esther V., *The Attalids of Pergamum*, Ithaca, New York, 1947

Haynes, Sybille, *Land of the Chimaera*, London, 1974

Herodotus, *The Histories*, translated by Aubrey De Selincourt, Harmondsworth, 1972

Jones, A. H. M., *The Greek City from Alexander to Justinian*, Oxford, 1940; *The Later Roman Empire*, Oxford, 1964; *The Decline of the Ancient World*, New York, 1966

Lloyd, Seton, *Ancient Turkey; A Traveller's History of Anatolia*, London, 1989

Martin, Roland, *Greek Architecture*, London, 1980

Pollitt, J. J., *Art in the Hellenistic Age*, Cambridge, 1986

Radt, Wolfgang, *Pergamon, Archaeological Guide*, Istanbul, 1984

Robertson, D.S., *Greek and Roman Architecture*, Cambridge, 1971

Stark, Freya, *Ionia, A Quest*, London, 1954; *The Lycian Shore*, London, 1956; *Alexander's Path*, London, 1958.

Stoneham, Richard, *Land of Lost Gods; The Search for Classical Greece*, London, 1987

Wycherly, R. E., *How the Greeks Built Cities*, New York, 1962

ACKNOWLEDGEMENTS

Photographs
A.E. Baker: pp. 1, 8, 12, 14, 20 (bottom), 24 (top), 31, 39 (bottom), 40, 46, 60, 62, 69, 81, 83, 89, 90 (top), 96 (top & bottom), 102, 105, 108, 109, 118, 121, 122, 124, 125, 130, 132, 135; Berge Aran: p. 56; Courtesy of the Archaeological Exploration of Sardis: p. 80; Courtesy of the Trustees of the British Museum: pp. 13, 20 (top), 49 (bottom), 98, 99, 100 (top left & centre), 101, 112, 113 (top & bottom); Deutsches Archäologishes Institut, Istanbul: pp. 26, 32; C.M. Dixon: pp. 39 (top right), 57, 63, 70, 76, 77, 128, 134; Clare Finlaison: p. 94; Ara Güler: pp. 5, 74, 90 (bottom), 117; Sonia Halliday Photographs: jacket photo and pp. 65, 78, 114; Staaliche Museen Zu Berlin: p. 33; Robert Harding Picture Library: p. 53.

The publishers would particularly like to thank Antony Baker for his photographs.

Plans
The following sources have provided the basis for certain plans in this book.

Ancient Civilizations and Ruins of Turkey, Professor Ekrem Akurgal, (Haşet Kitabevi, Istanbul, sixth edition, 1985): pp. 7, 18, 19, 27, 30, 36, 38, 45, 48 (top), 49 (top), 63, 65, 66, 68, 71, 94, 109, 111, 115, 120, 133; *The Architecture of Ancient Greece*, William B. Dinsmoor, (Batsford, London, third edition, 1950): p. 24 (bottom) as restored by Bacon and Clarke; p. 49 (top) as restored by Henderson; p. 75 as restored by Wiegand; p. 81 as restored by Butler; *Aphrodisias: City of Venus Aphrodite*, Professor Kenan T. Erim, (Century Hutchinson): p. 86 from an original drawing by Jeff Edwards; *Blue Guide: Greece* (A & C Black Publishers): p. 144 from original drawings by John Flower; *Ephesus*, Selahattin Erdengil, (Net Publishers, Istanbul): p. 51.

Every effort has been made to trace copyright-holders; it is hoped that any omission will be excused.

Author's acknowledgements
The author wishes to acknowledge his debt to Professor Ekrem Akurgal and the late Professor George Bean, whose pioneering works on the archaeological sites of Aegean Turkey were his guide when he first began exploring western Asia Minor.

INDEX